HIDDEN
BRITAIN

The crypt, Glamis Castle. *Image courtesy of the Earl of Strathmore and Kinghorne.*

HIDDEN BRITAIN

SECRET TUNNELS, LOST CHAMBERS AND UNKNOWN PASSAGEWAYS

ALVIN NICHOLAS

The History Press

Front cover images *left to right*: Bookcase door. *Courtesy of National Trust Images*; Baddesley Clinton. *Courtesy of National Trust Images/Andrew Butler*; The Marble Room, Harvington Hall. *Courtesy of Harvington Hall, www.harvingtonhall.com*; *bottom* 'Into the Light' *Shutterstock 139495202*
Back cover: The Marble Room, Harvington Hall. *Courtesy of Harvington Hall, www. harvingtonhall.com*

First published 2015
Reprinted 2016

The History Press
97 St George's Place,
Cheltenham, Gloucestershire, GL50 3QB
www.thehistorypress.co.uk

British Library Cataloguing in Publication Data.
A catalogue record for this book is available from the British Library.

ISBN 978 0 7509 5224 8

Typesetting and origination by The History Press
Printed by TJ Books Limited, Padstow, Cornwall

Contents

1

INTRODUCTION

If you could even guess the nature of this castle's secret, you would get down
on your knees and thank god it was not yours.

Claude Bowes-Lyon, 13th Earl of Strathmore

On a summer's day in 1793 a 22-year-old Walter Scott approached Glamis
Castle, ancestral seat of the earls of Strathmore. 'The hoary pile contains much
in its appearance, and in the traditions connected with it,' he later wrote. 'I
was conducted to my apartment in a distant part of the building. I must own,
that as I heard door after door shut, after my conductor had retired, I began
to consider myself too far from the living, and somewhat too near the dead.'[1]

Glamis Castle (*c.*1850).

Scott, writing in around 1830, happened to mention a secret chamber:

> ... a curious monument of the peril of feudal times ... the entrance of which, by the law or custom of the family, must only be known to three persons at once, viz. the Earl of Strathmore, his heir apparent, and any third person they may take into their confidence.

But the tale grew taller. Soon, it was said that the heir of Strathmore had to pass the night of his majority in the secret chamber, and that it was haunted. Meanwhile, sightings of a ghostly figure in an area of the battlements known as the Mad Earl's Walk were attributed to the 'Monster of Glamis', a horribly deformed rightful heir who was said to be imprisoned in a secret room to keep him out of sight and out of possession.

Fuel was added to the fire when a story began circulating about a workman who had stumbled upon a door near the chapel, behind which was a long corridor with *something* in it. Some said he came face to face with the prisoner. Others maintained he found skeletons, perhaps members of Clan Ogilvy who sought refuge at the castle after being defeated by the Clan Lindsay in 1445 (according to legend, an unsympathetic Lord of Glamis had them walled-up alive).

When Claude Bowes-Lyon, 13th Earl of Strathmore (grandfather of Elizabeth Bowes-Lyon, the late queen mother) heard about the incident, he is said to have immediately returned from London and, shortly after, the workman and his family were 'subsidised and induced to emigrate'.[2]

Several stories can be traced to the English singer and composer Virginia Gabriel. After a long stay at the castle in 1870, she returned 'full of mysteries' (or melodrama, depending on your point of view). Gabriel recorded a conversation with Lady Strathmore who, like her frustrated predecessors, was said to roam from room to room tapping on walls and taking up boards. At that time the factor, or estate keeper, was Andrew Ralston, a dour, no-nonsense, practical type who flatly refused – under any circumstance – to spend even a single night in the castle. When Lady Strathmore questioned him about the secret, he snapped, 'Lady Strathmore, it is fortunate that you do not know it and can never know it, for if you did you would not be a happy woman.'[3]

By the late nineteenth century the secret of Glamis Castle was the talk of Victorian high society, and it seems those who were closest to it revelled in the rumours. For example, when the 13th earl told his wife:

> My dearest, you know how often we have joked over the secret room and the family mystery. I have been into the room; I have heard the secret; and if you wish to please me you will never mention the subject to me again.[4]

... the effect, after it got out, was electric.

FAMILY
SECRETS

Keeping secret chambers secret makes perfect sense. After all, they can be used to hide valuables, or provide a refuge during a crisis.

At the core of Netherhall Mansion in Cumbria was a medieval pele tower (akin to a Scottish tower house). Built of dressed Roman stone, today it is the only part of the former seat of the Senhouse family to remain standing.

Here was a secret chamber, the location of which was a family secret. The historian and antiquary Allan Fea wrote:

> This room at Netherhall is said to have no window, and has hitherto baffled every attempt of those not in the secret to discover its whereabouts. Remarkable as this may seem in these prosaic days, it has been confirmed by the present representative of the family, who, in a communication to us upon the subject, writes as follows: 'It may be romantic, but still it is true that the secret has survived frequent searches of visitors. There is no one alive who has been in it, that I am aware, except myself.'

Writing in 1934, even priest-hole hunter Granville Squires could not prise the secret from the owners:

> Mr. G.J. Pocklington-Senhouse, who at present shares the secret with his brother, informs me that the origin of it is unknown. One cannot help speculating about this and wondering how near the secret has come to being revealed by those decorators and restorers whose attention every old house has needed at some period.

The last owner died without an heir and, shortly after, Netherhall was abandoned. By 1976 it was derelict following a fire and was subsequently condemned.

One explanation is that he was not as gloomy as he was made out to be. Although religious, Claude had a 'keen sense of the ridiculous'[5] and it was during his time as earl that talk of a secret peaked. The Bowes-Lyons' neighbour, Lord Crawford, thought he knew the answer. 'The Lyons talk freely about ghosts and invent stories to suit the idiosyncrasies of each guest,' he wrote. 'There is a secret: the secret is that there is no secret.'[6]

So was there ever a secret chamber at Glamis Castle? Almost certainly. The legend about the heir having to spend a night inside a haunted chamber may have come from an earlier one about Vale Royal, Cheshire[7] (the fact that Sir Walter Scott's 1825 novel *The Betrothed* features a similar haunted chamber could have aided its translocation to Glamis). However, there seems little reason to doubt Scott's original assertion – he writes plainly that he was told of a secret chamber and was well acquainted with Scottish castles. In addition, there were precedents. Netherhall Mansion, Cumbria, also had a secret chamber whose location was kept a family secret for generations (see p. 9), as were two priest holes at Sawston Hall, Cambridgeshire.

For all the conjecture, Glamis' core is medieval and massive. The earliest part now standing is the early fifteenth-century south-east wing with its round tower, the Great Round. To this was added a mid- to late fifteenth-century tower house (the Great Tower) – and tower houses are well known for architectural curiosities (see p. 154). Scott's friend, the antiquarian James Skene (1775–1864), thought the secret chamber at Glamis could be similar to the one at Castle Fraser (p. 157) and have a covert eavesdropping device or 'lug' – perhaps explaining the need to keep it a secret. Maybe it was an out of the way room, or an unusual dungeon. Certainly, if Glamis' secret chamber was anything like those found in other Scottish mansions, it would be located in the thick-walled heart. Accounts suggest a dreary, windowless room approximately 4.5m long by 3m wide; its supposed location, under the charter room.

In 1969, the 16th Earl, Timothy Bowes-Lyon, showed royal biographer Michael Thornton a bricked-up area near the charter room, claiming it led to the secret chamber. The claim appears to be supported by two entries in the autobiographical diary of Patrick Lyon, 3rd Earl of Kinghorne (1643–95), written between 1684 and 1689:[8]

The closet
within my
charter house

Agreed with the four masons in Glamis for digging down from the floor of the little pantry off the lobby a closet designed within the charter house there[.]

Later, he records additional work:

> Slopings in and
> about the
> charter house
> at Glamis

> I did add to the work before mentioned of a closet in my charter house several things of a considerable trouble as the digging through passages from the new work and through that closet again so that as now I have access off on floor from the east quarter of the house of Glamis to the west side through the low hall[.]

To what was he referring? Today's charter room is located at the top of the clock tower, but in the context of the two diary entries, this should be ignored.

What is known is this: between 1671 and 1689 Earl Patrick transformed the inconvenient and largely ruinous pile into the semblance of a mansion with a symmetrical front. Of significance here was a contract he signed with Alexander Nisbet in 1679 to undertake various alterations, including quarrying into the thick medieval walls and vaults to provide closets, chimneys, doorways and a prison.

In the angle between the south-east wing and the Great Tower, a small closet now leads to a larger closet, formed out of the thickness of the east wall of Duncan's Hall. This appears to be a closet made for Earl Patrick, and was likely discreet (if not secret). He also quarried through the thick north wall of the Laigh (i.e. lower) Hall (the so-called crypt) to create a mural passage.

The passage was not a secret. In Earl Patrick's time, there was no direct communication between the private apartments in the south-east wing and the public and state rooms in the north-west wing. Earl Patrick's solution was to dig out a passage in the thickness of the north wall, partition off the west end of the Laigh Hall and link the passage with Duncan's Hall and the private apartments. The 'little pantry off the lobby' (the floor of which was excavated to create a closet below) must have separated Malcolm's Room (formerly the High Lobby) and the Great Hall on the second floor.[9]

Shown as an open passage in eighteenth-century plans, alterations to the Laigh Hall made the mural passage redundant, and it was sealed. Soon after, the old passage became the 'secret chamber' in which, it was said, one of the lords of Glamis and the 'Tiger' Earl of Crawford played cards with the Devil on the Sabbath.

Case closed? Not quite. Virginia Gabriel claimed that some of the bedroom cupboards contained stones with rings, and several stories centre on the reputedly haunted Blue Room. Apparently, a closet off it concealed 'a well-known trap-door and a secret staircase leading to a corner of the drawing-room'.[10]

The stones remain a mystery, but the so-called Blue Room – now the Family Exhibition Room – is another of Earl Patrick's creations and is located on the

11

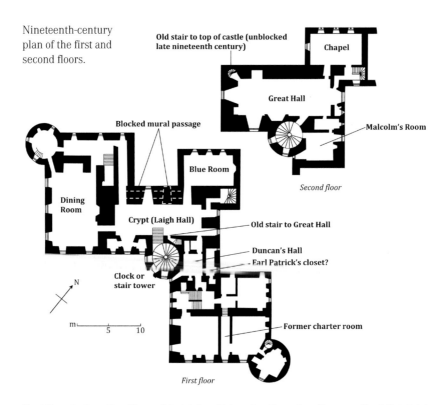

Nineteenth-century plan of the first and second floors.

Old stair to top of castle (unblocked late nineteenth century)

Chapel

Great Hall

Blocked mural passage

Malcolm's Room

Blue Room

Second floor

Dining Room

Crypt (Laigh Hall)

Old stair to Great Hall

Duncan's Hall

Earl Patrick's closet?

Clock or stair tower

N

Former charter room

m 5 10

First floor

first floor below the Chapel (which adjoins the Drawing Room – Earl Patrick's Great Hall). It shares part of the north wall of the Laigh Hall, and a not-so-secret late eighteenth-century stair to the Drawing Room adjoins its south-east corner. The trapdoor story might stem from a small medieval stair in the Drawing Room's north-west corner, blocked at the time of Gabriel's stay and likely labelled 'secret'.

What about the workman's 'discovery'? This story seems to stem from a period of restoration work in 1896 on the older parts of the castle under James A. Ferguson, estate architect and clerk of works to the Strathmore Estate from around 1889 to 1901. Two letters to the 13th Earl (who was indeed away at the time) detail progress and problems. However, the only alarming discovery was that two writing rooms off the Laigh Hall lacked proper ceilings and were in danger of collapse.

So it seems that some of the stories contained a grain of truth, but much was fabricated or at least embroidered. How much was real? No one alive knows. That is what makes a visit to Glamis and many other places in this book such a thrilling experience: the possibility, however remote, of a *discovery*.

HOW TO USE THIS BOOK

In most cases, it will be obvious from the text whether the said feature is genuine, conjectural or simply a far-fetched tradition. Occasionally, however, you will have to decide for yourself!

Most places and properties in the 'Amazing Places to Visit and Stay' section are to varying degrees accessible, but bear in mind that ownership and circumstances can change. Places and properties mentioned elsewhere may be accessible, long vanished or not publicly accessible (see 'Notes for Investigators'). In all cases, please check before visiting.

AUTHENTICITY

For those seeking the secret, the most important test of authenticity is to establish whether there was a *need* for secrecy. Of course, trouble came at various times and in many forms, but staunch adherence to the Roman Catholic faith during penal times is by far the most common affirming factor. The political correlate of Catholicism was Royalism, an additional clue.

Documentary evidence, signs of concealment (like a camouflaged entrance, locks or material to deaden sound), signs of furnishing, decoration and occupation help to build a picture. Very occasionally, when a secret chamber is uncovered after many years, artefacts are found that can provide valuable evidence – but be wary of corroborative details that sound too good to be true. They often are.

INTRODUCTION

2

PRIEST HOLES
& PASSAGEWAYS

In condemning us, you condemn all your own ancestors, all our ancient
bishops and kings, all that was once the glory of England – the island of
saints, and the most devoted child of the See of Peter.

St Edmund Campion (1540–81)

PRIEST HOLES

Old Catholic houses sometimes contain priest holes: dark, hidden spaces
where the grim past seems to commune with the present. The fact that they
are tangible, historic artefacts makes them fascinating and romantic places
to visit, especially when we know something of the trials and tribulations of
the people who built and used them.

The vast majority were created for Roman Catholic priests under Elizabeth I
(r. 1558–1603) and James I (r. 1603–25), with smaller versions for items used
to celebrate Mass. Some were used later and perhaps refurbished: during
and after the English Civil War, around the time of the Jacobite Risings
(1689–1745), and sporadically into the eighteenth century. A few were used
by smugglers.

Interesting as they are, priest holes rarely resemble the secret chambers
of fiction. In fact, historian Michael Hodgetts observed the 'average' priest
hole to be 'an almost featureless space, perhaps 8ft by 3ft and 5ft high, only
identifiable by its flooring and by its entrance, which is most often a trap-door
in a garderobe closet or other dark corner'.

That said, some are more complex than others – and a few (notably those
thought to have been constructed by Jesuit lay brother Nicholas Owen), display
great skill and ingenuity.

One of Owen's best can be found at Sawston Hall, Cambridgeshire[11] – for five centuries the seat of the Catholic Huddleston family, up until 1982. Their manor house was rebuilt to a courtyard plan following a fire in 1553 and the location of two of its three priest holes (of a basic hole-under-the-garderobe type) were, until recent times, a family secret.

The third is superb and bears all the hallmarks of Owen. It was probably built 1592–3, around the time he constructed a hide at Broadoaks Manor,[12] some 20km away (pp. 19–22). Located at the top of a pentagonal stair turret in the centre courtyard, it had but one purpose: to deceive. The circular stair terminates at a square landing with stout oak boards and nothing whatsoever suggests there is any space for a secret hiding place. There is just a wall and the roof. However, under the slope of the roof, where the wall meets the floorboards, two weighty boards can be lifted up to reveal a hole in a corner where the circular wall of the turret sweeps out from the flat wall of the long gallery.

The visual deception is completed by the fact that when put back in place, two-thirds of the boards overhang the stair so it appears there is little or no spare space. Three similarly shaped and equally spaced pieces of wood are nailed to the underside of the two boards. They slip neatly into cavities in the joists when the boards are replaced, preventing any sideways movement.

The hole runs sideways and down into the gallery wall to a secret chamber 2.5m long, 1.5m high and 0.5m wide. As one of Owen's priest holes, it is characteristically well equipped with recesses for candles or provisions, a stone seat and an externally masked hole for light and air. There is even a stone latrine. The careful concealment extends to the entrance to the turret in a wonderfully panelled gallery, where the wall is tapered to mask the thickness of the secret chamber above the door.

Owen clearly expended much time and energy building priest holes – and though he was the undisputed master of his art, he was by no means alone. But why go to the trouble of building them?

Britain, it must be remembered, was for much of its history a Catholic island, beginning in AD 597 when Pope Gregory of Rome sent Augustine of Canterbury to Christianize King Æthelberht and his Kingdom of Kent from their Anglo-Saxon paganism. The English Church adhered to Rome for almost a thousand years until 1534.

Coinciding with the religious ferment in Europe that began after Martin Luther's first challenge to the church in 1517, Henry VIII sought an annulment of his marriage to his brother's widow, Catherine of Aragon, after she failed to produce a male heir. When the Pope refused, Henry was furious. He split with the Catholic Church, extinguished all papal authority and founded the Church of England.

When Henry died, he was succeeded by his 9-year-old son, Edward VI (1537–53), the first English monarch raised as a Protestant. Edward was succeeded by his half-sister, Mary, who temporarily reversed the Reformation and took England back into the Catholic Church (burning many Protestants along the way and acquiring the nickname 'Bloody Mary').

In 1558, Mary was succeeded by her Protestant half-sister Elizabeth (1533–1603), and the politico-religious pendulum swung the other way. To make matters worse, Catholic plots to overthrow the queen led to severe 'penal laws', including the famous 'Act against Jesuits, Seminary Priests and other such like disobedient persons' of 1584. Catholics were forbidden to hold services and any priests who remained in the country risked death. Meanwhile, those who gave refuge to priests risked imprisonment, the confiscation of their property, torture – or worse. Post-Reformation persecution in Scotland followed a parallel trajectory to that of England and Wales, arriving in waves following the Scottish Parliament's decision to break with Rome in 1560.

Those who clung to the 'old faith' and refused to attend Protestant services were known as recusants, and in addition to torture and imprisonment, they faced heavy fines and excommunication, and were deprived of privileges of citizenship such as free travel.

Founded in 1534, the Society of Jesus, whose members are called Jesuits, formed the backbone of the Counter-Reformation. Native Catholic gentlemen were conveyed to seminaries abroad where they were trained and ordained as Jesuit priests. They were then smuggled back to Britain to carry on their work as part of an underground network that required the construction of priest holes in the houses of principal Catholics (the families of which were often connected by blood ties and other relationships). To oppose the perceived threat, the Elizabethan regime mobilised a mercenary-like corps of priest hunters or 'pursuivants', a secret service run by the queen's spymaster, Sir Francis Walsingham (c.1530–90)

Elizabeth I was succeeded by James VI of Scotland, the son of Mary Queen of Scots, who now became James I of England (r. 1603–25). Despite Catholic hopes of tolerance, penal laws were strengthened, especially after the Gunpowder Plot of 1605. Following a period of relative tolerance during the reign of Charles I (r. 1625–49) the situation changed after the predominantly Puritan Long Parliament challenged the king's authority in the 1640s. Further suffering coincided with the Wars of the Three Kingdoms (of which the English Civil War is the best known), and the period following the abolition of the monarchy under Charles I, known as the Commonwealth (1649–60).

After the Restoration under Charles II in 1660, persecution eased considerably. However, a short period of persecution occurred between 1678 and 1681 after Titus Oates fabricated a 'Popish Plot' that maintained Charles was to be murdered and his Roman Catholic brother James (1633–1701) installed on the throne. Indeed, restrictions against Roman Catholics were still in place until full emancipation in 1829.

Priest holes could, quite literally, be the difference between life and death. How did it feel to be holed up in one?

ST NICHOLAS OWEN (C. 1550–1606)

A Jesuit lay brother, Owen built numerous high-quality priest holes, often containing emergency exits and, whenever possible, his hides were linked up so they could be used in conjunction with one another. Born in Oxford, he was probably a carpenter and mason by trade and often travelled under the name of Little John, a reference to his short stature and one of several aliases. For seventeen or so years Owen worked under the Jesuit priest Henry Garnet (1555–1606), and his priest holes, for which he was paid in food and lodgings only, were much in demand.

According to Father John Gerard:

> He was the immediate occasion of saving the lives of many hundreds of persons, both ecclesiastical and secular ... He laboured in all shires and in the chiefest Catholic houses in England ... He was so careful that you should never hear him speak of any houses or places where he did make such hides, though sometimes he had occasion to discourse of the fashion of them for the making of others. He did much strive to make them of several fashions in several places, that one being taken might give no light to the discovery of another.[15]

Owen was first arrested in 1582 or 1583 after the execution of Edmund Campion for publicly proclaiming the latter's innocence. He was arrested again in 1594, and this time tortured (illegally). In 1606 Owen was again captured and tortured – this time to death – after being starved out of one of his own hides at Hindlip Hall, Worcestershire.[16] One report said, 'they tortured him with such inhuman ferocity that his stomach burst open and his intestines gushed out'.

The main primary sources for the subject are two books by the Jesuit priest, John Gerard (1564–1637). His *Narrative* and *Autobiography*[13] are thrilling accounts of the dangerous, cloak-and-dagger world of a Roman Catholic priest in Elizabethan England.

Gerard was born in Derbyshire of Lancashire parents. After training and ordination in Rome he was smuggled back to England, mostly working in the Midlands and Eastern counties. Over nine years he had many adventures, often escaping by the skin of his teeth. Tall, dark and impeccably well-dressed, he passed himself off as a gentleman hunter. A 'wanted' notice drawn up by the 'cruellest Tyrant of all England', investigator Richard Topcliffe, described him in less flattering terms:

> Jhon Gerrarde, ye Jhezewt is about 30 years oulde Of a good stature sumwhat higher then Sr Tho Layton & upright in his paysse and countenance sum what stayring in his look or Eyes Currilde heire by Nature & blackyshe & not apt to have much heire of his bearde. I thincke his noase sum what wide and turninge Upp Blubarde Lipps turninge outwards Especially the over Lipps most Uppwards toword the Noase Kewryoos in speetche If he do now contynewe his custome ... And in his speetche he flourrethe & smyles much & a falteringe or Lispinge, or dooblinge of his Tonge in his speeche.[14]

Broadoaks Manor near Saffron Waldon, Essex, was the scene of his most memorable adventure.

★ ★ ★

Back in the sixteenth century this E-plan, moated Tudor house was the home of the staunchly Catholic Wisemans, a family who were often in trouble with the authorities. A few months prior to Gerard's arrival, Broadoaks was raided and an old priest named Richard Jackson was found in a 'secret place between the walls'. According to the report, weaponry was found in a vault behind a door, consisting of 'three horsemen's armours, seven other armours, two muskets and two cullivers, bows and arrows, a jack and a shirt of mail'.[17]

The house was under surveillance, and special measures were needed before Gerard could take up residence. Protestant servants were replaced with Catholics, though the family retained the services of a Protestant servant named John Frank (a mistake – he was a spy).

A week or so before his arrival, Gerard was almost caught. He had travelled to London and his lodgings at Golding Lane were raided, his movements having been relayed to the authorities by John Frank. Fortunately, Gerard was out visiting his superior, Father Henry Garnet. Four people were arrested at Golding Lane, including Gerard's servant. The authorities sent a summons to Mr Wiseman, who then travelled to Golding Lane. He was arrested and sent to the Tower.

The authorities sent Frank to visit Mr Wiseman in the hope of obtaining information on Gerard's whereabouts. Gerard, meanwhile, had returned to Broadoaks to discuss events with Mrs Wiseman and to prepare for Easter services. Frank was sent after him – ostensibly with letters from Gerard's servant and from Mr Wiseman to his wife. Upon his return to London, Frank reported Gerard's whereabouts. Then, on Easter Sunday 1594, he returned to Broadoaks bearing yet another letter. In the early hours of Monday (1 April), two magistrates had the house surrounded.

Frank ran downstairs and made a show of resisting the pursuivants whilst Gerard and Jane Wiseman quickly hid incriminating evidence. Gerard made for an older, well-stocked secret hiding place, furthest from the secret chapel at the top of the house and near the Great Chamber. However, Mrs Wiseman insisted he went into a secret hiding place under a false hearth that had been recently built by Nicholas Owen. Quickly, she gathered some biscuits and quince jelly and secured the priest in his hole.

The account of the search appears in Gerard's *Autobiography*, and is best told by the author himself:

> The searchers broke down the door, and forcing their way in, spread through the house with great noise and racket. They then took to themselves the whole house, which was of a good size, and made a thorough search in every part, not forgetting even to look under the tiles of the roof.

Using candles, the pursuivants examined every dark corner, but:

> Finding nothing whatever, they began to break down certain places that they suspected. They measured the walls with long rods, so that if they did not tally, they might pierce the part not accounted for. Thus they sounded the walls and all the boards, to find out and break into any hollow places there might be.

On the second day (2 April) the pursuivants probed the fireplace through which his hide was entered. Gerard could hear the discussions above:

> Might there not be a place here for a person to get down into the wall of the chimney below, by lifting up this hearth?
> 'No' answered one of the pursuivants. 'You could not get down that way into the chimney underneath, but there might easily be an entrance at the back of this chimney.'

After two days, the search party had drawn a blank. Later, Gerard recalled:

> Here was I in my hiding-place. The way I got into it was by taking up the floor, made of wood and bricks, under the fireplace. The place was so constructed

that a fire could not be lit in it without damaging the house; though we made a point of keeping wood there, as if it were meant for a fire.

After dark, the false fireplace presented a new and unexpected danger:

> Well, the men on the night watch lit a fire in this very grate and began chatting together close to it. Soon the bricks which had not bricks but wood underneath them got loose, and nearly fell out of their places as the wood gave way. On noticing this and probing the place with a stick, they found that the bottom was made of wood, whereupon they remarked that this was something curious. I thought that they were going there and then to break open the place and enter, but they made up their minds at last to put off further examination till next day.

Gerard had been lucky – but was his luck about to run out?

> Next morning, therefore, they renewed the search most carefully, everywhere except in the top chamber which served as a chapel, and in which the two watchmen had made a fire over my head and had noticed the strange make of the grate. God had blotted out of their memory all remembrance of the thing. Nay, none of the searchers entered the place the whole day, though it was the one that was most open to suspicion, and if they had entered, they would have found me without any search; rather, I should say, they would have seen me, for the fire had burnt a great hole in my hiding-place, and had I not got a little out of the way, the hot embers would have fallen on me ... The searchers, forgetting or not caring about this room, busied themselves in ransacking the rooms below, in one of which I was said to be. In fact, they found the other hiding-place which I thought of going into, as I mentioned before. It was not far off, so I could hear their shouts of joy when they first found it. But after joy comes grief; and so it was with them. The only thing that they found was a goodly store of provision laid up ... They stuck to their purpose, however, of stripping off all the wainscot of the other large room. So they set a man to work near the ceiling, close to the place where I was: for the lower part of the walls was covered with tapestry, not with wainscot. So they stripped off the wainscot all round till they came again to the very place where I lay, and there they lost heart and gave up the search. My hiding-place was in a thick wall of the chimney behind a finely inlaid and carved mantelpiece. They could not well take the carving down without risk of breaking it. Broken, however, it would have been, and that into a thousand pieces, had they any conception that I could be concealed behind it. But knowing that there were two flues, they did not think that there could be room enough there for a man.

Against all the odds, and as a testament to Nicholas Owen's skill, Gerard had evaded capture.

Remarkably, though much of the old house has disappeared, survivals include the north-west portion that comprises the main block and part of the north wing, which still contains the long, low secret chapel on the upper level and the 'unsafe' hide. It also contains the Owen-built hide in which Gerard hid.

To create his hide, Owen removed the tiles from the fireplace and made a false hearth, beneath which he burrowed downwards through solid brickwork. The secret chamber adjoins the large living room below and is located high up and to the right of a Renaissance fireplace. It is 0.6m wide and 1.7m tall at its highest point, with two brick seats or steps immediately beneath the hearth, as well as a recess for a latrine in one corner.

PASSAGEWAYS

'There existed, within the old Red Lodge at Woodstock, a Labyrinth, or connected series of subterranean passages,' wrote Sir Walter Scott in his novel, *Woodstock*. Substitute 'passages' for 'drains', however, and the romance vanishes – with few exceptions, secret passageways turn out to be old drains.

Secret passageway traditions go hand in hand with old churches, abbeys and monasteries. It is said that a passageway beneath this church led to the local pub!

That does not mean they are uninteresting. The main drain of a monastry was often a magnificently built structure: stone vaulted with a paved base (like the great drain of Paisley Abbey, Renfrewshire). A main drain at Baddesley Clinton Hall, Warwickshire (p. 91) was converted into a secret hiding place, and redundant drains might easily be reused for stealthy travel or escape.

They can also be revealing. Typical is the example at Chenies,[18] a much changed and diminished Tudor manor house in Buckinghamshire. An 'escape tunnel' in the gardens turned out to be a finely engineered medieval drain connecting long-vanished buildings – a clue that enabled Channel 4's *Time Team* to piece together the Tudor layout.

Garderobes (latrines) were sometimes converted into hides, and former drains reveal their original use. They might also explain legends about 'secret ways' from priest holes. At Cleeve Prior Manor House,[19] Worcestershire, a priest hole was constructed under the floor of a small closet room on the first floor. It has a heavy trap door made of floorboards and a well-preserved bolt for locking it from on the inside. The secret chamber itself is around 1.8m long, 1.2m wide and 4.5m deep. It appears to be genuine, and is said to have hidden Thomas Bushell, a philosopher and farmer of His Majesty's Mines in Wales, who supplied money to Charles I's army at Oxford at a time when Parliamentary forces held the Tower Mint. The proximity of the adjacent parish church inevitably gave rise to a rumour that there was a passage between the two, and the story was taken seriously enough for Worcestershire antiquarian, John Humphreys, to test it. Of course, he found nothing. The rumour stems from a blocked-up, ground-level garderobe outlet. Timber-framed Harborough Hall,[20] near Kidderminster, dates to the seventeenth century and had two secret hiding places. One, behind the kitchen chimney, was reached from the floor above. Another is in the garret at the back of the house, next to the chimney. When it was discovered in the early nineteenth century, it was found to contain old books. A garderobe chute running down from the hide was examined by the owner. He found a brick-vaulted tunnel at its base, and decided to explore it. Upon entering the tunnel he was forced to stoop, and when his candle went out and mysteriously re-lit after a few yards he 'took the hint' and retreated! Priest-hole hunter Granville Squires pointed out that the tunnel runs diagonally across the yard and straight to a lake a short distance away, proving conclusively that it was a drain. He also said:

> This fact in no way detracts from its reputation as a hiding place, but adds to it, for it is far more likely that something like this would be adapted for escaping purposes than that a tunnel of this size could be dug and vaulted in brick in secret.

A classic 'secret' passageway exists at Burton Constable Hall,[21] a rambling Elizabethan pile in Yorkshire. Entered through a modern trapdoor, it is possible to stand in the 18m-long passage. It runs between the floorboards of one corridor and the ceiling of a corridor below, and terminates in an octagonal, windowless room. Almost certainly this was leftover space, and not part of the original design.

SECRET TUNNELS

Of course, excavating a tunnel of any length requires time, manpower and resources of a magnitude that make secrecy nigh on impossible. Nowhere is this more apparent than at Welbeck Abbey, Nottinghamshire,[22] where the eccentric and reclusive William John Cavendish-Bentinck-Scott, 5th Duke of Portland (1800–79) created an extensive network of underground tunnels and chambers during the nineteenth century – a feat that required 1,500 men and £2 million. Near High Wycombe, Buckinghamshire, the extravagant Francis Dashwood, 15th Baron le Despencer (1708–81) paid numerous poverty-stricken farm workers a shilling a day to dig his spectacular network of chalk and flint caverns, now known as the Hellfire Caves.[23] The rock from this philanthropic endeavour was used as foundation stone for a new road between High Wycombe and West Wycombe.

Sally ports were sometimes hewn from difficult solid rock to provide secret escape routes from castles or to harass besieging troops, but secret and not-so-secret tunnels almost always exploit natural advantages like pre-existing caves, mines or exceptionally amenable geology.

Some of Britain's most interesting tunnels are to be found in Nottingham. Hundreds of labyrinthine, man-made caves, chambers and other features are cut into the underlying sandstone here, some dating back many hundreds of years, and parts of which are yet to be explored (p. 87.) At Reigate Castle, Surrey, there are similar subterranean chambers and passages (p. 65) and St Andrews Castle, Fife (p. 132) boasts a remarkable mine and countermine, both dug during the siege of 1546–47. However, Britain's most impressive castle tunnels are to be found in the soft chalk beneath Dover Castle, Kent. To find out more, turn to p. 53.

3

GOTHIC DISCOVERIES,
CUNNING DEVICES

'The secret chamber is unrivalled even by the haunted house for the mystery and romance surrounding it,' wrote Allan Fea in his 1901 book, *Secret Chambers and Hiding Places*. Secret chambers intrigue and delight, but spurious additions and a haze of folkloric tradition have deterred serious study. Granville Squires' book, *Secret Hiding Places* (1934), was the first attempt. He frequently encountered problems:

> Several years ago an iron box containing papers of no value was found in a recess under the floor of a cupboard at Hassop Hall, near Bakewell. When I heard of the account of this find, given with much corroborative detail, it had grown to be a box of jewels valued at £15,000 found behind a moveable partition, behind which was a passage to an old monastery.

Glamis aside (see *Introduction*), it is not difficult to find other examples. Take the case of a panel in the Blue Room at seventeenth-century Chelvey Court, Bristol. According to a story, it flung open whilst being dusted (frightening the cleaner so much, she fled). A nineteenth-century antiquarian wrote to *Notes and Queries* stating that he had heard about the panel as well as a priest hole in another part of the house, and somewhat sceptical of 'tall tales about secret doors and passages', had visited.[24] Unfortunately, his conductress said she had hastily closed the panel and could no longer locate the spring by which it opened, and, 'For some unexplained reason she was evidently disinclined to have any further investigation made in this matter.'

The case of a two-storey former farmhouse called Church Living (located north-east of St Winfred's Church in Branscombe, Devon) is also typical. With an unusually complex architectural history, the house – now split into two – dates mainly from the late fifteenth and early sixteenth centuries but has some thirteenth-century features. It was rumoured to be full of hiding places and, being so close to the church, it was naturally thought a secret passageway ran between the two. A local tradition maintained that there were 'lost' cellars – or even another house – *under* Church Living.

When the local Victorian artist and diarist Peter Orland Hutchinson visited (he called it 'The Clergy'), his 'chatty' hostess, a Mrs Somers, showed him a trapdoor immediately inside the entrance that could be pushed up from below to reveal a small room lacking any communication with the rest of the house and lit by a slit window above the door. He was also shown a hole in one of the thick walls and a void that descended from somewhere near the roof to the ground. When a stone was dropped into the hole, it was heard to rattle and come out at the bottom. Mr Hutchinson was then conducted to several spots where the stone floor sounded hollow when stamped upon, and Mrs Somers said that her husband had recurring dreams about the entrance to an 'underground house' being near the dairy window. Haunted, he was, by the thought of an undiscovered secret chamber!

Many accounts speak of sealed-up, secret rooms – sometimes containing skeletons – where ancient yet recognisable objects crumble to dust when touched. A ghost story is often thrown in for good measure (priest holes were often closed up because superstitious servants believed they harboured ghosts).

Bovey House, Devon,[25] is a largely sixteenth-century manor house with medieval origins. During the nineteenth century a secret room complete with chair, table and the remains of tapestry was discovered in the easternmost of its three gables. Within the bounds of the property there is an extremely deep well in which a skeleton was found, and it contains a square recess in solid rock many metres down, said to have been used as a Royalist hiding place.

The sixteenth-century manor house of Bourton-on-the-Water, Gloucestershire, was a rambling pile of many gables. Prior to its demolition in the nineteenth century, a concealed door was found on the second floor landing, behind which was a 2.5m square chamber. Apparently, it contained a chair and table. A priest's cassock hung over the back of the chair. An antique teapot, cup and silver spoon stood on the table, but the tealeaves had long crumbled to dust. On the same floor were several supposedly haunted rooms including the Chapel, a room with a vaulted ceiling known as the Priest's Room and a mysterious room that had been locked for many years, known as the Dark Room.[26]

In his *Memoirs of the Life and Actions of Oliver Cromwell* (1740), Francis Peck tells a similar story. In 1708, whilst installing a new chimney at the now ruinous Minster Lovell Hall, Oxfordshire, a large underground vault was found. It was said to have contained the skeleton of a man sitting at a table. Before him was a book, pen and paper; and in another part of the room lay a cap, 'all much mouldered and decayed'. The remains were rumoured to be those of Richard III's favourite, Lord Lovell. He famously fled the Battle of Stoke Field in 1487, never to be seen again.

Though unquestionably entertaining, most stories of this type are so ludicrous they can be dismissed out of hand. Some, however, stem from genuine antiquities. Danby Hall, near Middleham, Yorkshire, was the seat of the

Royalist Scrope family. Here a 3m by 1.8m, 1.8m-high secret chamber was discovered in a chimney stack in the early nineteenth century. It contained useable swords, pistols, saddlery and harness, believed to have been stored for the Jacobite Rising of 1715. Compton Wynyates provides another example.[27] Located in a secluded Cotswold hollow, it has been described as 'the most beautiful Tudor house in England'. Tradition has it that whilst playing as a child in the south-west tower in about 1770, Lady Frances Compton fell against a plastered wall that gave a hollow sound. Upon investigation, a chamber behind was found to contain the skeleton of a woman and two children. True or not, in the very same tower there is a small room at the top – thought to have been a secret chapel and known as the Priest's Room, approached from the Council Chamber below via three staircases. Inside, there is a priest hole under a garderobe. Just occasionally, tradition points the way.

OPEN SESAME!

In addition to antiquities, ghosts and skeletons, tradition frequently furnishes secret chambers with hidden mechanisms. Take this letter to the nineteenth-century Catholic journal, *The Rambler*, for example:

> In the State Room of my castle is the family shield, which on a part being touched, revolves, and a flight of steps becomes visible. The first, third, fifth, and all odd steps are to be trusted, but to tread any of the others is to set in motion some concealed machinery which causes the staircase to collapse, disclosing a vault some seventy feet in depth, down which the unwary are precipitated.

If only! At Penhow Castle, South Wales,[28] the ancient Seymour Chamber staircase has a trick or stumble step designed to impede an attacker's progress, and there are movable stairs that give access to priest holes. However, there is nothing like the killer stair of the unknown castle. Equally implausible is a tradition that the magnificent fireplace in the late seventeenth-century Gilt Room of Tredegar House, South Wales, swung around to reveal a passage when the now vanished tongues of two gargoyles were pulled in unison. Visitors who peer into their gaping mouths and examine the fireplace will see no evidence of a former contrivance. Everyone loves the story just the same.

We can take comfort from the fact that some of the curiosities beloved of nineteenth-century writers such as Sir Walter Scott *do* exist. Aston Hall, Birmingham, has a nineteenth-century chair that swings out on hinges to reveal a cavity (p. 102). The hinged portrait in the novel, *Woodstock* (1826), is based on a real one at Lyme Park, Cheshire (p. 118) and Lord Halifax created three secret hiding places for his children to play in at Garrowby Hall, Yorkshire,[29] one of which was entered through a similar hinged portrait.

Moveable panels can be found at Clarke Hall, Wakefield,[30] Boughton House, Northamptonshire (p. 84), Low Hall, West Yorkshire[31] and Chichester Cathedral, West Sussex (p. 70).

The alleged existence of a spring-operated panel at Chelvey Court, Bristol, was discussed earlier. Stonyhurst, Lancashire (p. 122), is said to have had a secret hiding place behind a fixed bookcase, the back of which opened via a secret spring. The closest approach to such things are to be found at Ufton Court, West Berkshire (p. 44) and Mapledurham House, Oxfordshire (p. 60), both of which contain hides that were opened via ingenious (and ancient) spring bolts.

'Gib' doors with real or dummy books are a much-loved feature and were popular additions to grand houses in the eighteenth and nineteenth centuries. Examples may be seen at Killerton House, Devon,[32] Highclere Castle, Berkshire (p. 50), Scotney Castle, Kent (p. 54), Felbrigg Hall, East Anglia,[33] Ingatestone Hall, Essex (p. 76), Oxburgh Hall, Norfolk (p. 78), Hampton Court, Herefordshire (p. 83), Belvoir Castle, Leicestershire,[34] Hazelwood Castle, West Yorkshire (p. 135), Lauriston Castle, Edinburgh (p. 152) and Balfour Castle, Orkney (p. 165).

Scottish castles have more than their fair share of curiosities. For example, the 'laird's lug' at Castle Fraser, Aberdeenshire, is supposed to have allowed the laird to hear what was going in the hall. Similar devices were installed elsewhere (see pp. 157–61). A wonderfully eccentric mechanism was installed at early twentieth-century Carbisdale Castle in the Scottish Highlands.[35] The Lower Gallery contained a number of Italian marble statues, one of which was connected to a mechanism. When rotated, a secret door opened below the Great Staircase.

4

Amazing Places
to Visit and Stay

SOUTH-WEST ENGLAND

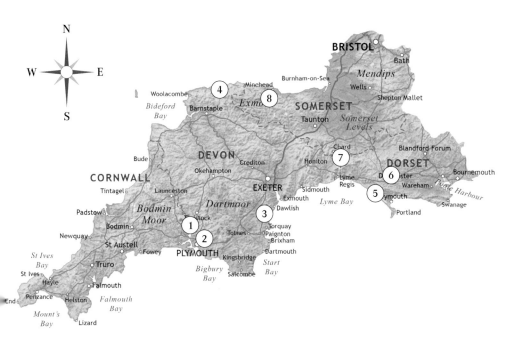

South-West England is synonymous with romantic manor houses, coastal castles and hidden smuggler's coves. Steeped in history and tradition, the region abounds with antiquities, curiosities and mysteries.

1. COTEHELE HOUSE CORNWALL

Cotehele, 'ancient, large, strong and fayre', served as the principal seat of the aristocratic Edgecumbe family from 1353 to 1947. A product of growth rather than plan, this rambling, dimly lit house is one of the least-altered in Britain. Its rooms are festooned with period oak furniture, rich tapestries and ancient armour. It even has a spyhole.

What lies within? The cloam oven at Cotehele House, Cornwall.

Today's Tudor structure was largely built between 1485 and 1560, and is mostly the work of Sir Richard Edgecumbe (c.1443–89) and his son, Sir Piers (1477–1539). Sir Richard was among the disaffected gentry who declared themselves against the crown after rumours that Richard III ordered the murder of the sons of his dead brother, Edward IV. However, following the defeat of rebel forces led by Henry Stafford, Duke of Buckingham, Sir Richard was outlawed and forced into hiding. Eventually, he was tracked to Cotehele by the king's much feared local agent, Sir Henry Trenowth of Bodrugan. As the net closed, Sir Richard cut a sentry's throat and made a dash for the River Tamar. Then, as Sir Henry's men closed in, he placed a stone in his cap, cast it into the water and hid nearby.

Having outwitted his pursuers, Sir Richard fled to Brittany where he befriended and joined forces with Henry Tudor. He went on to fight at his side at the Battle of Bosworth Field (where Richard III was defeated and killed, enabling Henry to take the crown). Upon his triumphant return, Sir Richard erected a chapel at Cotehele, on the very spot where he had hidden.

According to tradition, a hoard of silverware was hidden in the house. In 1642, just prior to the outbreak of the Civil War, a letter dated 1618 was discovered in a false-bottomed chest. It was enigmatic, and spoke of 'strong chests', 'hidden secrets' and 'enemies'.

Now it so happens that in the kitchen there is a great cloam oven, 2.1m across, a little less than 1m high and oval in shape, necessarily constructed within a massive stone wall. Above this, and somewhere within the thickness of the wall, there is said to be a secret chamber that was investigated by nineteenth-century antiquarians.

What did they discover? A dusty old bridle! According to a rumour, a mason beat them to it. He had chanced upon the secret chamber whilst working on improvements to the house – perhaps at the time of the oven's installation. Upon his death he left his daughter a large sum of money that no one could account for.

In *More Famous Homes and Their Stories* (1900), Alfred Henry Malan claimed he had 'opened out' a similar cloam oven secret chamber in a sixteenth-century manor house, the location of which is not disclosed:

> The little hiding-place was very ingeniously entered. There was a hole ten feet up the wide chimney, and invisible from below, reached by a short ladder being brought and pushed up the chimney; and from the manhole a passage ran down behind the chimney-back into a domed chamber below. This was seven feet by five feet six inches, and five feet high, absolutely dark, except for a small keystone drawing inwards; and it had so well proved itself to be a secret chamber that successive modern tenants had no notion of its existence, until the containing wall became ruinous, and an accident chanced to reveal it.

Often, unwarranted romantic significance is attached to mundane voids like smoking chambers, service areas and redundant space. On the other hand, such things could be converted to secrecy if required – and hides off fireplace flues occur elsewhere.

If there is any truth to our tale, it points to a small chamber off the flue, somewhere above the cloam oven. Is it there? At present, no one knows. Two small ovens are shown in a plan of 1731, yet the cloam oven is not. Originally, there was a fireplace here, and the thickness of the wall meant a cloam oven could be installed (probably in the later part of the eighteenth century). In a cloam oven, smoke, having nowhere else to go, billows out into an adjacent chimney flue – so the flue from the old fireplace was retained. These days it is closed off. There are no plans to open it.

St Dominick, near Saltash PL12 6TA; National Trust, open part year, gardens open all year.

2. Warleigh House Devon

'A seat both pleasant and profitable; for standing near the Tamar side, and having a park, and fair demesnes, belonging to it, it wants no variety, which sea or land can yield.' So wrote John Prince in his great work of 1701, *Worthies of Devon*. The description remains accurate.

Overlooking the beautiful River Tamar amidst ancient coastal oak woods, this largely sixteenth-century, E-plan country house probably occupies the site of a twelfth-century house built for Sampson Foliot (whose manor of Tamerton became Tamerton Foliot). In 1741, Warleigh became the property of the Radcliffe family and was remodelled shortly after. From 1825–31 it was remodelled again, this time under the renowned Plymouth architect, John Foulston.

The north wing contains a pre-sixteenth-century, stone-vaulted cellar and tradition speaks of a secret passageway from the great hall to the nearby riverbank. If there is anything to the story, it is certain to be an old drain. Of course, ascertaining whether drains were ever used as secret passageways is difficult, if not impossible.

Occasionally, there are clues. If a passage exists, it has an equivalent at Irnham Hall, Lincolnshire[36] – the former seat the resolutely Roman Catholic Thimbelby family. Here in 1929, a 1.5m-high vaulted underground passage was found under a flagstone in the great hall hearth. It runs to a small chamber beneath a beech tree some 50m or so away, its exit covered by a stone slab (now under turf). Since it slopes downhill, it was probably a drain. However, there is a high-quality secret hiding place on the first floor of the oldest wing (unconnected to the passage). Since a hide was required, the drain might well have been converted into an emergency bolt hole, or even a hide in its own right.

Tamerton Foliot, Plymouth PL5 4LG; private house, bed and breakfast accommodation.

3. Old Forde House Devon

Over the years, Old Forde House has received many distinguished guests. In 1625, Charles I visited on his way to inspect the fleet at Portsmouth and stayed overnight. Other visitors included Sir Thomas Fairfax and his lieutenant general, Oliver Cromwell (1646), as well as William of Orange (1688).

Beginning as one of Torre Abbey's grange farms, the older part of the building (to the rear) is attributed to John Gaverock, a former abbot's steward who acquired the manor in 1540 following the Dissolution of the Monasteries. The present E-plan manor house dates to 1610 and was built by the Reynell family.

Old Forde House retains an interior with finely carved panelling, an oak staircase, great oak doors and magnificent, finely decorated plaster

Stair leading to the Long Room or Great Chamber, Old Forde House.

ceilings. Other features include a sliding step in a short flight of stairs on the first landing, beneath which there is said to be a deep cavity and another stairway leading out of the house to the Aller Brook.

Renovations rendered the secret stairway inaccessible, but it is likely to be a drain, perhaps converted to a bolt hole. Nearby, in the middle of the landing floor, a short floorboard can be taken up to reveal a shallow recess with compartments created by wooden partitions – somewhere to hide valuables, perhaps, or important papers.

Over the main staircase there is a very large window within a thick stone wall. The top part has been blocked up, but it is hardly noticeable. On the other side small opaque panes have been put in, and between the two lies a mysterious hollow space.

Brunel Road, Newton Abbot TQ12 4XX; Teignbridge Council, tours of the house are held during the summer months and private group bookings can be arranged at weekends.

4. Chambercombe Manor Devon

A curious tale is attached to this late medieval manorial farmhouse. During roof repairs in 1865, a former owner noticed a blocked-up window without a corresponding room. He knocked through a wall and discovered a four-poster bed – upon which was a skeleton.

The remains were thought to belong to the daughter of an eighteenth-century tenant who was a ship-wrecker. According to the story, he unwittingly lured a ship carrying his daughter on to the rocks of nearby Hele Bay and, grief-stricken, had her body walled up. Today, the so-called Haunted Room is open for public inspection.

Chambercombe Lane, Ilfracombe EX34 9RJ; Chambercombe Trust, open part year, offer overnight stays.

5. Old Fleet Church Dorset

Smuggling was rife in Dorset and the Isle of Wight, particularly during the eighteenth century. *Moonfleet* by J. Meade Falkner is a gripping yarn about a boy named John Trenchard who finds an opening into a tomb in Fleet churchyard (a few miles west of Weymouth), reputed to be a repository for pirate treasure:

> ... it was not more than twenty yards or thereabouts; and then I came upon a stone wall which had once blocked the road, but was now broken through so as to make a rough doorway into the chamber beyond. There I stood on the rough sill of the door, holding my breath and reaching out my candle arms-length into the darkness, to see what sort of place this was before I put a foot into it ... I knew that I was underneath the church, and that this chamber was none other than the Mohune Vault.

Surrounded by a graveyard next to an atmospheric salt marsh, Old Fleet Church is now the mortuary chapel of the local landowning Mohun family (does the name sound familiar?). Only the medieval chancel remains, since the rest of the church was destroyed by a violent storm in November 1824.

Following the publication *Moonfleet* at the end of the nineteenth century, a gravedigger came across a curious stone-vaulted passage. However, a funeral was underway so he could not investigate. The discovery was related to a Dr Goodwin from Weymouth, who some years later found the time to look into the claim. A buried slab in the churchyard was raised and beneath was found a vaulted passage some 1.5m high, just under 1m wide and some 30m long, sloping towards the sea. One end adjoined a burial vault and the other was blocked with stones.[37] The tunnel appeared to have been built to drain the vault but, given easy access from the sea, could well have been used by smugglers (at Kinston Church, a few miles east of Bournemouth, a tomb near the church was used as a smuggler's repository).

Meade Falkner was surprised by the discovery. Although *Moonfleet* used local geography, the details were fictional.

Chickerell, Weymouth DT3 4EE; accessible via public footpaths.

6. ATHELHAMPTON HALL DORSET

◇◇◇

Described as a 'most glorious relic of the Dorset of bygone years', Athelhampton Hall was built around 1490–95 by Sir William Martyn, a prosperous sheep farmer and local administrator. This imposing, L-plan manor house boasts a two-storey entry porch, an atmospheric great hall and immaculate walled gardens.

What oak-panelled hall would be complete without clattering duellists (the Great Hall), the odd shadowy monk and an inevitable grey lady? Athelhampton claims all – and more. From the Great Hall an ante-room leads to the sixteenth-century Great Chamber via two Tudor archways.

It was built by Robert Martyn, Athelhampton's owner from 1525–50 and boasts a trio of mullioned windows depicting heraldic images. Within the west

An imposing relic of bygone times: Athelhampton Hall.

Cosy and inviting: the Great Chamber, Athelhampton Hall

wall, hidden behind panelling, a concealed spiral staircase leads to the Long Gallery above, and to the cellar. This is the famous 'secret passage', the stairs of which are associated with the ghost of a former pet ape. Depicted bound in chains, 'Martyn's ape' became the family crest.

Athelhampton, Dorchester DT2 7LG; private house open to the public, open part year.

7. THE CHOUGHS HOTEL SOMERSET

◇◇◇

According to tradition, there were several secret hiding places here. This interesting L-plan house, now a hotel, probably dates to the early seventeenth century.

Years ago a petrified bird in a miniature 'coffin' was discovered in a recess – a curious artefact thought to be connected with witchcraft. The famous bird has become something of an heirloom, and is solemnly entrusted to successive occupants.

A seventeenth-century gravestone offers a good excuse for a tipple. Set into the fireplace, it is said that any attempt to take a flash photograph of the relic is destined to fail!

8 High Street, Chard TA20 1QB.

8. DUNSTER CASTLE SOMERSET

The wood-cloaked hill from which the castle takes its name has been occupied for over a thousand years. Following the Conquest, an early keep was given to Sir William de Mohun, a noble of Norman descent. The Domesday Book records, 'William himself holds Torre, and there is his castle. Aluric held it in the time of King Edward.'

The oldest part of the present castle is the twin-towered gateway to the Lower Ward, built in the early thirteenth century by Reynold de Mohun II. Adjoining this is an oubliette, a pit or dungeon into which prisoners were thrown via a trapdoor. It is said that nineteenth-century workmen found human remains here.

Dunster passed to the Luttrell family in 1485 and remained in their hands for eight generations. The extant H-plan Jacobean mansion was built in 1617 by George Luttrell (1560–1629) and incorporated much of the older fabric.

Thomas Luttrell (1583–1644) initially supported Parliament during the Civil War, but when the king's forces took Taunton and Bridgewater his Royalist cousin, Colonel Francis Wyndham, persuaded him to surrender. In May 1645, Charles I ordered Thomas Luttrell's son George to accommodate a 15-year-old Charles II (as Prince of Wales) so he could 'encourage the new levies', it being 'not known at Court that the plague, which had driven him from Bristol, was as hot in Dunster town, just under the walls of the castle'. [38]

Dunster Castle

November 1645 saw Colonel Robert Blake lead a Parliamentarian force against the castle, and it was besieged for 160 days. However, the war was turning against the king and Colonel Wyndham was persuaded to accept an honourable surrender. Then, in 1650, Cromwell ordered the destruction of the defensible castle. Fortunately, the Jacobean mansion was spared.

Rumours speak of secret stairways and escape passages but, to date, nothing has come to light. A *known* hide is located off the King Charles Bedroom, and is traditionally associated with the prince's stay. However, the bedroom was not named until the nineteenth century and Prince Charles was accompanied by loyal troops. In addition, he probably stayed in an adjacent room (from which there was no access to the hide).

To the left of the bed a modern concealed door is kept open so that visitors can peer inside a narrow, 25cm-wide passage. Concealed by a false wall, it leads off to the right (behind the bed) and terminates after 3.5m. At the end there is a recess to the left and what appears to be a stone seat. Originally, it was covered with sixteenth- or seventeenth-century Romayne panels – some fragments of which are displayed.

The space is too narrow to have been a closet or garderobe. It appears to be a priest hole – but who built it? The Luttrells do not appear to have been Catholics, but there were intriguing family connections. For example, in July 1558, Catherine, the eldest daughter of Sir John Luttrell (1518–81) married Sir Thomas Copley, a Catholic convert who had been Princess Elizabeth's Latin tutor. What is more, in 1621, George Luttrell I threatened to cut his daughter Elizabeth out of his will if she should marry a recusant or even the son of one. 'She nevertheless married, in that year, Thomas Arundel of Chideock in Dorset, a member of a noted Roman Catholic family.'[39]

That there was a family secret is self-evident – but we may never know the details.

Minehead, Dunster TA24 6SS; National Trust, open part year.

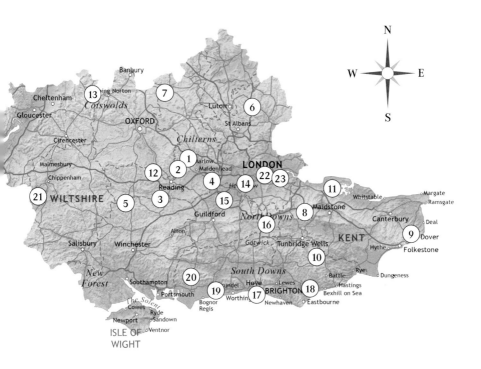

With famous strongholds and royal palaces, stately homes and moated manor houses, southern England and London are an antiquarian's paradise. Here we explore secret chambers, tunnels and forgotten places at the heart of British history.

1. BISHAM ABBEY BERKSHIRE

This timeless jewel stands in picturesque grounds on the south bank of the River Thames. During the reign of Henry III, the manor of Bisham was granted to the Knights Templar and they established a preceptory (headquarters) here. Surviving structures from that time include the Great Hall, around which the present Tudor mansion was constructed.

   Following the suppression of the order, Edward II took over the manorial rights. During the Scottish Wars of Independence he used the manor house as a place of imprisonment for Queen Elizabeth of the Scots (the wife of King Robert the Bruce), along with her stepdaughter Princess Marjorie and her sister-in-law, Lady Christine of Carrick.

In 1335 the manor passed to William, 3rd Baron of Montacute (1301–44). William had been a supporter of Edward II and was instrumental in the arrest of the king's murderer, Rodger Mortimer. In 1337, Edward III rewarded Montacute with the earldom of Salisbury, and in that same year he obtained a licence to found a magnificent priory for Austin canons next to his home, Bisham Priory. A total of six earls of Salisbury were buried here, including 'Warwick the Kingmaker', Richard Neville (who through marriage became the Earl of Salisbury and whose son-in-law was Richard III).

Bisham Priory was dissolved in July 1557 and then refounded as a short-lived Benedictine abbey. It was finally dissolved in June 1558 and, of this priory, nothing remains.

Bisham was granted by Henry VIII to Anne of Cleeves and later conveyed by her to Sir Philip Hoby (1505–58) in exchange for his house in Kent. Sir Philip erected the Great Dining Hall and made a number of other modifications. On his death, the manor passed to his half-brother, Thomas Hoby (1530–66). It was he who completed the house and erected the imposing brick tower.

Princess Elizabeth was kept in the care of the Hobys at Bisham for several years during the reign of her half-sister, Mary. She supposedly drank from the holy well (later named after her) and planted a mulberry tree that may still be seen today.

Of the legends associated with the house, by far the best known concerns Thomas Hoby's wife, the energetic and highly educated Lady Elizabeth Hoby (1528–1609). A quick-tempered perfectionist, she is said to have beaten to death her youngest son, William, for constantly blotting his copybook. Her repentant ghost walks the grounds, wringing its hands in despair (she may be identified with the help of her cold, staring portrait in the Great Hall). Apparently, a set of blotted and untidy notebooks were found hidden in a recess during nineteenth-century alterations.

Several nineteenth-century sources mention a secret chamber high in a thick wall and hidden behind the tapestry of one of the bedrooms, its chimney connected to the hall chimney to conceal smoke from its fireplace. The chamber, it is said, was reached via a small concealed door to the right of a fireplace bearing the Hoby coat of arms.

This was indeed the case. In the sixteenth century, the roof of the magnificent fourteenth-century Council Chamber was sealed by the insertion of another floor during Hoby alterations. Reached via a ladder to a small door high in the north wall of the Tapestry Room, it naturally became known as the 'secret chambers' (but they could not have been very secret). The Tapestry Room is so called because of its fine tapestries depicting the story of the biblical book of Tobit, part of the Apocrypha. Now displayed at the Winnipeg Art Gallery, Canada, they were commissioned around 1530 and are attributed to the Flemish artist Bernard van Orley (c. 1488–1541). Upon their removal a pointed, late fourteenth-century window was uncovered.

Bisham, Marlow SL7 1RT; English Sports Council, residential sports centre hosting a wide variety of events and activities, open all year.

2. LADYE PLACE BERKSHIRE

◇◇

Once regarded with superstitious awe, a subterraneous vault here echoes the literary secret chamber – atmospheric, elaborate and the setting for a high-stakes plot.

In the time of the Confessor, the manor of Hurley in the Thames Valley was held by Asgar (or Easgar), Master of the King's Horse. After the Norman Conquest, Asgar was forced to cede the manor to Geoffrey de Mandeville (d. *c.* 1100), a Battle of Hastings veteran, first Constable of the Tower of London and one of the Conqueror's tenant-in-chiefs. It was Geoffrey who, between 1085 and 1087, founded Hurley Priory as a cell of Benedictine monks subject to St Peter's, Westminster. The moated monastic complex remained in Benedictine hands until 1536, at which time it was dissolved and the lands passed into secular ownership. Today, the only visible monuments are the remains of a rectangular moat (best preserved on the north side where it survives as a linear pond), fishponds and various buildings grouped around a courtyard and partly occupying the site of the original cloister garth.

Vaulted undercroft, Ladye Place.

After passing through several hands in 1545 John Lovelace (d. 1558) acquired the priory. Around 1600 his son, Richard (a buccaneer in his youth), built a new manor house called Ladye Place. 'His mansion,' says Macaulay, was 'built out of the spoils of Spanish galleons from the Indies,' and 'rose on the ruins of a house of our Lady, in that beautiful valley, through which the Thames, not yet defiled by the precincts of a great capital, nor rising and falling with the flow and ebb of the sea, rolls under woods of beech round the gentle hills of Berkshire.'

Ladye Place fell into dereliction in the early nineteenth century and the fixtures and furnishings were auctioned off. It was demolished in 1837 and replaced by a largely Victorian successor of the same name.

Located within grounds belonging to the newer house is the only part of its predecessor to have survived. Built in around the sixteenth century, it is a vaulted undercroft (a cellar or storage room) that occupied a space beneath the Great Hall. Typically for an undercroft of the period, the I-shaped compartment is largely brick-lined and sunk some feet below ground level. It is divided into four bays by square vault-supporting brick piers placed centrally down the compartment. The space was lit by a pair of three-light mullioned windows in the south wall and two similar, single light windows – one in the west wall of the projecting wing and another in the east wall of a closet at the southern end (the top of the L).

John Lovelace, 3rd Baron Lovelace (1641–93) used the undercroft for secret meetings when he and a group of like-minded nobles plotted the overthrow of the Catholic James II (calling for the Protestant Prince of Orange to take the throne as William III). Macaulay wrote:

> Beneath the stately saloon, adorned by Italian pencils, was a subterraneous vault in which the bones of the monks had sometimes been found. In this dark chamber some zealous and daring opponents of the government held many midnight conferences during that anxious time when England was impatiently expecting the Protestant wind.

Papers that brought about the Glorious Revolution were reputedly signed in a dark recess at one end (the closet). After William had taken the throne, Lovelace gave him a tour.

It has long been said that plotters covertly entered the undercroft via a secret tunnel – a brick-lined main drain from the manor house to the moat, located near a building opposite the parish church called The Cloisters (originally part of the refectory of the Benedictine priory). Parts of the drain were 'cleaned out' by retired Royal Engineer, Colonel Charles Rivers-Moore.

Colonel Rivers-Moore purchased Ladye Place in 1924. The small country estate comprised of the main residence, 20 acres of land, secondary residences and cottages. Keenly interested in the estate's history, the colonel and his wife, Barbara, joined the Berkshire Archaeological Society and determined to investigate.[40]

In term of field work, little had been done previously. The couple were particularly intrigued by a fourteenth-century reference to Edward the Confessor's sister Edith having been buried at Hurley Priory. Her ghost – a grey lady – was supposed to haunt the place.

But where to dig? By chance, a dry summer revealed the outline of the Lovelace mansion, part of which stood on the remains of the old priory. However, beyond investigating the recorded history and a trial pit, there was little activity. Then, in the spring of 1930, Mrs Rivers-Moore's brother – a London based doctor – arrived for a stay. One day, he surprised everyone by claiming to have had a 'vision' of a brown-habited monk in The Cloister's dining room (Colonel Rivers-Moore called the building 'Paradise').

It seems the apparition had an eye for interior design. The doctor made a remark about a fireplace not in keeping with the rest of the house, and the monk motioned with a hand and three times said, 'Sweep it away.' At that moment the doctor had another vision: a much older fireplace with a great oak lintel. The next day, Mrs Rivers-Moore had the offending fireplace removed. Behind it was found a fireplace in keeping with her brother's vision.

Between 1930 and 1938 psychic-inspired archaeological discoveries attracted much media attention and, towards the end of the period, veteran psychic archaeologist Frederick Bligh-Bond (1864–1945) became involved. Bond famously investigated Glastonbury Abbey and claimed he was 'guided' in his efforts by the architect of Edgar Chapel and by dead monks.

In August 1930 'communications' were received about a well in the vicinity of the east end of the church in which, it was alleged, a monk had thrown stolen jewels. It was not long before a debris-filled well was found in the area described. However, Hurley is low-lying and flood prone. Shortly after digging began, water was struck at the level of the Thames (3m down). The attempt was abandoned shortly after.

In 1933 they again attempted to reach the bottom – this time with the assistance of the Marlow Fire Brigade. Unfortunately, an emergency call came through. Save for a broken teapot of a fairly recent date, no relics were discovered. A final attempt in 1937 yielded but one relic of interest – a battered brass candlestick engraved with the letter 'K' that probably belonged to the last tenant of Ladye Place, Gustavus Adolphus Kempenfelt (whose brother Admiral Kempenfelt went down at Ryde in HMS *Royal George*, 29 August 1792). A well in the courtyard was similarly barren.

As for the grave of Edith, Colonel Rivers-Moore's report of 1938 said, 'Although nothing positive has come to light to identify this the workers found a base of hard core surrounded by traces of tile flooring ... This could hardly have been the base of any altar in this position but may well have formed the base of some shrine.'

According to tradition, a tunnel runs between the site of the priory and Ye Olde Bell Inn (some 300m south along Hurley High Street, past an early fourteenth-century tithe barn). The inn claims a founding date of 1135, but the present building dates to the late fifteenth century. A cupboard, behind which was a staircase, was a reputed point of access.

The Olde Bell, Hurley High Street, Hurley, Maidenhead SL6 5LX. Ladye Place Crypt lies on private land and is at present unsafe. However, The Olde Bell is an ideal base for a walk around Hurley and along the Thames River Path.

3. UFTON COURT BERKSHIRE

Treasure was hidden in a secret chamber here. Approached via an avenue of fine oaks, Ufton was (and remains) isolated. In fact, one former owner got lost in the woods and had to be rescued by local villagers. Lady Elizabeth Marvyn was so grateful she left money in her will of 1581 for an annual dole of bread and cloth to the poor of Ufton – still given out from a window in the Great Hall. The promise of a curse on any landlord who breaks the tradition ensured its survival!

This irregular, E-plan Elizabethan manor house was built around a late fifteenth-century hall house that belonged to Francis Lovell, 1st Viscount Lovell (1454 to c.1487). It was probably used as a hunting lodge (his main residence was Minster Lovell Hall, Oxfordshire). Lovell, whose heraldic symbol was a silver wolf, along with Sir William Catesby (1450–85) and Sir Richard Ratcliffe (d. 1485) were Richard III's closest supporters. The trio feature in a doggerel from the time:

> ... the Catte, the Ratte and Lovell our dogge
> rulyth all Englande under a hogge.

The 'hogge' was, of course, Richard (he had a white boar on his crest). The king wasted no time tracking down the writer – a Wiltshire man named Sir William Collingbourne. He was hung, drawn and quartered for his efforts. In 1485 Lovell fought at Richard's side at the Battle of Bosworth Field and following the king's defeat fled, went into hiding and disappeared.

The Roman Catholic Perkins family owned Ufton from 1581 to 1769 – a span of seven generations, each one headed by a Francis Perkins. In 1586, a watch was placed on the house by a local tailor named Roger Plumpton. It was soon raided following his report, which read:

> There resorteth unto the dwelling house of the said Ffrauncys Parkyns a certain unknowen person which is commonly lodged in a cocke lofte or some other secrett corner of the howse and is not commonly seene abroade, but cominge abroade he weareth a blew coate which person soe unknowen he vehemently suspecteth to be some seminary priest; for that on divers

Wenesdayes, Frydayes, & other festivall dayes, he hath seene most of the familye, one after another, slipping upp in a secrett manner to a highe chaumber in the toppe of the howse, and there continewe the space of an hower and a halfe or moore and this examinatt, harkening as neere as he might to the place, hath often heard a little bell rounge, which he imagineth to be a sacring bell, wherby he conjectureth that they resort to heare masse. Divers other unknown persons suspected to be papists resort to the house of the sayde Ffrauncys Parkyns in secrett manner, sometymes by daye some-tymes by night.[41]

Local Justices of the Peace searched 'the studdy, clossette and other secrett places of the howse', examining letters and books. On this occasion, no incriminating evidence was found. Thirteen years later on the night of 17 July 1599, Ufton was raided with greater success under Sir Francis Knollys Junior (*c.* 1550–1648). Two warrants were issued, one for the apprehension of Father John Gerard following his escape from the Tower of London and one for his superior, Father Henry Garnett. The second warrant referred to a great treas-ure hidden in the house, suspected to belong to 'ill-affected persons', and to be destined for clandestine purposes.

In the end, it was decided to raid the house at daybreak. After much knocking the company were let in. Francis was away but his brother, Thomas, appeared

The site of a dawn raid: Ufton Court.

Behind the staircase from the ground floor, entered through a small closet, is a small oratory. The religious monograms 'I.H.S.' and 'M.R' have been painted on the rough boarding covering the walls.

holding a light. Accompanied by his wife, he offered to escort the men around the house. Thomas obligingly opened all the doors bar one (he claimed he did not have the key). Not satisfied with this, the searchers kicked it open to reveal 'divers relickes and popishe trashe' including holy water, half-burnt candles, pictures and various other items for Mass.

All the while one of the searchers – an Edmund Duffield – had been absent. He reappeared and announced he had 'found the nest'. Perkins was duly summoned, but claimed to know nothing of it. Candles were brought and a priest hole opened. Inside were two chests. One contained bags of gold, the other silver plate and they were so heavy they had to be raised with a rope. Once the chests had been hauled up they were placed in a closet in the next chamber and their contents placed on a table. The haul was valued at £1,300.

The following day the treasure was to be taken to the nearby home of Sir Humphrey Foster, but, not finding him at home, Sir Francis and the others took the gold to Reading Abbey, leaving his servant, Sir Humphrey, to bring the silver in a cart later. At some point £751 16s 7d in silver was stolen. Later, the family tried to recover their losses through the courts but were unsuccessful.

Of the four hides at Ufton, the one that held the treasure is a hole in a dark corner of a small landing on the first floor. It occupies an unused space next to the centre chimney stack and is 1m long by 50cm wide and almost 3m deep.

When the hide was rediscovered many years later it was found to contain an ivory figure and two old guns (but alas, no treasure). It was covered by a broad oak plank (now displayed inside the hole) and retains its original rough ladder. On the underside of the trapdoor there is a rare wooden spring bolt of a type that occurs at two other hides at Ufton and at two more at Mapledurham (p. 60).

The bolts could be the work of a single man, perhaps Owen. The bolt at Ufton was activated via a loop-ended nail that was attached to some string. The other end of the string was attached to the wooden bolt. By lifting the nail and pulling it to the right it acted as a lever, pulling the string and releasing the bolt.

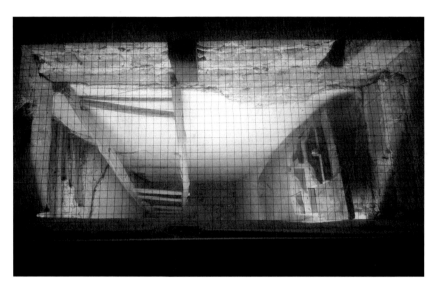

The priest hole in which treasure was hidden

Door to gable hide. The well-preserved bolt no longer has its wooden spring. It was released via a concealed string allowing the door to swing outwards.

There is another priest hole on the same floor in the north-west corner of the house, located in the floor of a small closet by the side of a fireplace and reached via a modern trapdoor. The shaft leads down past the ground floor to the cellars, from which it is bricked off. When first discovered it had two chambers, the upper one, with a wooden floor, 1m or so below the trapdoor.

On the attic floor are two gable hides, both fitted with secret doors. They are probably the 'coche loftes' spoken of by Roger Plumpton. Each door had a spring and bolt arrangement similar to that of the priest hole on the landing. One is entered in the corner of a small attic room and has a small triangular door made of plastered timber on a wooden pivot, just under 1m above the level of the floor under the angle of the roof. The bolt is well preserved, but no longer has its wooden spring. It was released via a concealed string allowing the door to swing outwards. The space within could have concealed many but would have been uncomfortable due to the angles and joists. There was no other exit. The other gable hide is situated on a landing and has a door with a similarly intact wooden bolt. This door opens to the floor, but at 2m, is taller. It leads to a chimney stack, around the corner of which is another large garret space sufficient for ten or more people.

Green Lane, Ufton Nervet RG7 4HD; Ufton Court Educational Trust, educational centre for children and young people. Not generally open to the public but hosts events and open days.

4. WINDSOR CASTLE BERKSHIRE

Windsor Castle is famous for its long association with the British royal family, its immense size and for its spectacular architecture. The original castle was built in the eleventh century following the Norman Conquest. Since the time of Henry I, it has been used by successive monarchs and is the longest occupied palace in Europe.

Naturally, the world's largest inhabited castle dominates the village – even (some say) below the surface. That tunnels exist under Windsor is well known: from the cellars of the Horse and Groom pub, the Crooked House, Nell Gwyn's House and the Carpenter's Arms (where a bricked-up tunnel produces 'spooky' noises). However, none of these tunnels communicated with the castle – and they were not very secret.

A *genuine* secret tunnel is associated with the Curfew Tower. Standing 30m tall and with 4m-thick walls at its base, it was built under Henry III during a series of defensive improvements between 1227 and 1230.

In the floor of an office off St George's Chapel a double wooden trapdoor gives access to a wide, stone-lined passage beneath the Curfew Tower. Forty rock-cut steps lead under the now dry moat, the passage taking a higher level towards a collapsed end. This was a sally port – a secret exit that allowed defending troops to mount a surprise attack.

In the basement of a shop at 2 Curfew Yard, Thames Street, there is a blocked passage that is said to have led to the Curfew Tower via the sally port. It could simply be a drain, but its proximity to the tower is intriguing.

Windsor, Berkshire SL4 1NJ; The Crown Estate, open all year.

Nineteenth-century antiquarian discoveries in Windsor Castle included the mouth of a well in the Round Tower (top), the subterranean sally port (bottom left) and an old culvert drain (*London Illustrated News*, 11 June 1887).

5. Highclere Castle Berkshire

Surrounded on all sides by a stunning Capability Brown landscape, the opulent seat of the earls of Carnarvon is famous for its association with the lost tomb of Tutankhamun and, more recently, ITV's *Downton Abbey*.

The Herberts inherited the estate from the Sawyer family. Sir Robert Sawyer (1633–92) was Attorney General during the reign of Charles II and a friend of the celebrated diarist Samuel Pepys. He bequeathed Highclere to his daughter, Margaret, the first wife of the 8th Earl of Pembroke, Thomas Herbert. The estate then passed to their second son, Robert Sawyer Herbert (1693–1769) and then to Robert's nephew, Henry (1741–1811) – later created 1st Earl of Carnarvon. It was he who remodelled the earlier house to create a square neo Georgian mansion, uncovering, it is said, 'secret passageways' behind old walls (what became of them is not recorded).The exotic, Jacobean-style house of today was built for the 3rd Earl by Sir Charles Barry (1795–1860), architect of the Houses of Parliament. In the opulent Library, amidst shelves of leather-bound books, a hidden door leads to the exquisitely ornate Music Room.

Highclere houses an exhibition exploring the 5th Earl of Carnarvon, George Herbert's famous archaeological expeditions that in 1922 culminated in the discovery of Tutankhamun's treasure-laden tomb. Many of the finds on display were secreted in obscure locations around the house including in 'secret' cupboards located in the wall thickness between the double doors of the Drawing Room and Smoking Room (rediscovered by the family in 1987).

When in 1923 Lord Carnarvon died from blood poisoning brought on as a result of an infected mosquito bite, it was famously blamed on the 'mummy's curse'. Lord Carnarvon's son, the 6th Earl, said publicly that although he 'neither believed nor disbelieved' the curse, he would 'not accept a million pounds to enter the tomb of Tutankhamun'.

Highclere Park, Newbury RG20 9RN; private house open to the public, open part year and opening times may vary.

6. Knebworth House Hertfordshire

Knebworth has been the seat of the Lytton family since the reign of Henry VII. Today's imposing, Tudor-style country house represents one wing of a red-brick, mid-sixteenth-century courtyard house – 'a large quadrangle, with a gothic archway flanked by two huge square towers and backed by a large watch-turret'.[42] The west wing forms the present house and contains an exceptionally well-preserved seventeenth-century hall.

In an effort to save money, Elizabeth Barbara Bulwer-Lytton (1773–1843) had the other three sides demolished in 1811 and remodelled the remainder. Her son, Edward Bulwer-Lytton (1803–73), was a prolific writer and poet who coined such phrases as 'the pen is mightier than the sword' and the infamous opening line, 'It was a dark and stormy night'. He confessed that the spirit of romance in his novels was largely inspired by the old house, 'in itself a romance':

> The antlers of stags, so vast that their genus seems to have vanished from our parks and forest, like things before the Ark, were ranged below the grim gothic masks that served as corbels to the beams of the lofty ceiling that domed the desolate banquet-hall. Trap-doors and hiding places, and a kind of oubliette called the 'Hell-hole,' presented themselves to the respect of the young poetess.[43]

In particular he recalled a long gallery that terminated in gloomy, ancient tapestry-draped 'haunted rooms'. In an adjoining room belonging to one of the square towers of the gateway was a curious trapdoor, beneath which was a dungeon-like void without windows or doors.

'How could I help writing romances,' he wrote, 'when I had walked, trembling at my own footstep, through that long gallery, with its ghostly portraits, mused in those tapestry chambers, and peeped, with bristling hair, into the shadowy abyss of Hell-hole?'

Why was it built? The Lyttons were Protestants, so they did not need priest holes (Elizabeth I stayed in 1571). Edward believed that one of his ancestors, Sir William Lytton MP (1586–1660) named the chamber after a Westminster eatery called 'Hell' in which he and others were confined following Pride's Purge of 1648 (the removal from Parliament of MPs willing to treat with Charles I).

Given the Lyttons' lack of either Roman Catholic or strong Royalist sentiments, the chamber probably had mundane origins. Located in the north wing in the westernmost tower, it could have been a cellar, a drain, or a hiding place for valuables. Since the north wing was one of those pulled down in 1811, it is unlikely we will ever know.

Knebworth SG3 6PY; private house open to the public, open all year except during events.

7. CLAYDON HOUSE BUCKINGHAMSHIRE

<><><><><><><><><><><><><><><><><><><><><><><><><><><><><><><><><><><><><><><><><><>

Notable for its lavish, rococo state rooms, Claydon House was built between 1757 and 1771 for Ralph, 2nd Earl Verney. There was a pre-Conquest house here, but by the time of the Domesday Survey, the manor belonged to the Peveralls, a family of Norman descent.

Since 1620 Claydon has been the ancestral seat of the Verneys and the nearby church contains a number of family memorials, including that of Sir Edmund Verney (*c.* 1590–1642), chief standard bearer to Charles I. Sir Edmund was killed at the Battle of Edgehill on 23 October 1642. According to family lore only his severed hand was found, still gripping his standard. The pre-eighteenth-century house was notable for having an unusual Civil War-era secret hiding place in the great central chimney, entered via a trapdoor in its muniment room.

Claydon is today owned by the National Trust, but its ancestral owners continue to live in the south wing.

Middle Claydon, near Buckingham MK18 2EY; National Trust, open part year and opening times may vary.

8. IGHTHAM MOTE KENT

<><><><><><><><><><><><><><><><><><><><><><><><><><><><><><><><><><><><><><><><><><>

With its half-timbered façade and little hump-backed bridge, this gorgeous architectural gem is one of the most complete examples of a medieval moated manor house in Britain. Ightham retained its medieval appearance despite many later alterations, largely because they were made using local materials and were sympathetic to the ancient building.

Constructed around three courtyards, the oldest part of the house dates to the fourteenth century and contains the hall, chapel, crypt and two solars. The gatehouse was added about 1480 and the main courtyard was enclosed by a further wing containing a new chapel in around 1520.

Six and a half centuries of weathering and atmospheric pollution had taken their toll, and four years after the house was gifted to the National Trust in 1985 they began an ambitious, £10 million conservation programme that involved dismantling, recording and reconstructing much of the building.

What would they find? It is recorded that Sir Christopher Alleyn 'kept a vile, papistical house' and, in September 1585, Ightham was raided. Alleyn's servants were questioned and Lady Alleyn's chamber searched for 'relics'. Despite this, no priest holes came to light.

Sir William Selby (1532–1612) bought Ightham in 1591. Upon his death, it passed to his nephew, another Sir William, and the house remained with the family for three centuries. The Selbys of Ightham were Protestants, and any priest holes could have been removed before they took up residence, or obliterated during alterations.

Ightham's many interesting features include an early porter's squint and a cupboard with a curious and familiar tradition. One Boxing Day in the nineteenth century, workmen removed some panelling at the Buttery end of the Great Hall. They found a wall, behind which was a cupboard. When they opened the door, they were surprised to find a young woman's skeleton – sitting upright in a chair!

Mote Road, Sevenoaks TN15 0NT; National Trust, open all year.

9. DOVER CASTLE KENT

Britain's most impressive castle tunnels are to be found here. Located high above Dover's white cliffs, this strategically important fortification has a long history of occupation and use. The site was probably fortified during the Iron Age, before the Romans built a flint-rubble lighthouse here (the remains of which can still be seen next to the church of St Mary in Castro). The Saxons erected a 'burh' (a defended place) and following William the Conqueror's victory at Hastings in October 1066, his forces marched on to Dover. The Normans strengthened the existing fortifications by erecting a motte and bailey. The Great Tower, the inner curtain and a portion of the outer curtain were constructed between 1180 and 1189 under Henry II and additional work to the outer curtain was implemented under King John.

Cut through soft chalk, tunnels beneath the castle can be divided into medieval, Napoleonic and Second World War sections. The eerie medieval tunnels (on the landward side) are a consequence of King John's refusal to accept and abide by the Magna Carta (in theory imposing limits on the king's power over his subjects). The First Baron's War (1215–17) followed, and rebel barons asked Prince Louis of France (later King Louis VIII) to take the English throne. Louis arrived in England and eventually besieged Dover ('the key to England'), which at the time was held by Hubert de Burgh (c. 1160–1243), a staunch ally of the king. Louis made for the north gateway and managed to capture the barbican. Meanwhile the castle's defenders dug a mine under the gate, which brought down part of the eastern tower, forcing the attackers to retreat.

To counter the threat of an attack from Napoleonic France a much larger network of secret tunnels was begun on the seaward side in 1797, housing secure underground barracks for up to 2,000 soldiers. The Second World War led to the large-scale modification and extension of the network and it was from here that Operation Dynamo – the evacuation of 338,000 Allied soldiers from the beaches of Dunkirk in May 1940 – was planned and implemented.

Castle Hill, Dover CT16 1HU; English Heritage, open all year but times and dates may vary.

10. SCOTNEY OLD CASTLE KENT

◇◇◇

Christmas 1598 was cold and wet, but for Father Blount and his loyal assistant, Bray, the miserable weather was the least of their worries ...

With its stunning gardens and tranquil river moat, this wonderful fortified house seems a world away from high drama and death-defying escapes. Overlooked by a nineteenth-century Salvin mansion, Scotney Old Castle is gorgeous, despite being largely ruinous.

It was begun during the Hundred Years War by Conservator of the Peace in Kent and Sussex, Roger de Ashburnham, probably around 1378–80, a period when a French invasion seemed imminent. It took the form of an irregular stone quadrangle fortress built on two islands in the River Bewl (a tributary of the Teise), connected via a causeway, and upon which a gatehouse was erected. Only one of its four round towers survives – the iconic, machicolated Ashburnham Tower.

Connected to this is the still extant Elizabethan brick manor house built by the Catholic Darrell family, within which is a fine, probably seventeenth-century staircase. Immediately to the east of the house are the ruins of the old hall block, originally medieval, and remodelled by William Darrell in the 1630s (dismantled during the construction of the 'new' castle).

On the second floor landing of the manor house there is a small doorway in the landing wall. In times past this was a secret doorway, leading then as today to a small room under the eaves, the floor of which is raised above the landing level. A pursuivant would be instantly drawn to this and assume that the difference in level concealed a hiding place – but it was a deceit. They would find nothing beneath the floorboards here.

On one side of this chamber there is a low door in a thick wall, leading to another space under the eaves. It is possible there were escape routes from here to the upper and lower levels of the house.

At the foot of the door there is an archetypal 'cunning device'. A huge block of oak, supported underneath by stout wooden runners can be made to slide back under the step to reveal a short, sloping shaft leading to a stone-lined secret chamber off the flue of an old kitchen chimney. It is a tiny space, 1.2m high, 1m wide and 1.5m long. Upon its discovery in the mid-nineteenth century, it was found to contain an anti-Catholic proclamation.

Two independent accounts record a raid at Scotney,[44] one of which was written by Thomas Darrell's son, William Darrell (d. 1639), a child in the castle at the time of the events recorded. He called the aforementioned secret chamber 'the hole under the stairs', since a stairway formerly continued to the hall block and over the hide.

Father Richard Blount (c. 1565–1638), later the head of the Jesuits in England, was headquartered here from 1591–98, and the house was searched twice. Blount had gone abroad to study and take holy orders, but like others, he undertook the perilous journey back to England to secretly minister to remaining Catholics.

The first raid lasted a week. Blount and his brave servant, a fellow named Bray, were hidden in the aforementioned secret chamber with a stock of provisions. Two Justices of the Peace, along with a pursuivant (and other hired thugs) sent everyone away from the house save for the maidservant and the children. Then, they simply waited (a week was usually enough).

Blount and Bray were confined to their hell-hole for seven long days. Something had to give, so the two men concocted a ruse. Bray left the hide via one of its bolt holes and gave himself up, telling the pursuivants he had been hiding in another part of the house. They led him away for interrogation and Blount escaped. Since there was no evidence against Bray, and since he was quite obviously not a priest, he was released and he rejoined his master.

On a bitterly cold December night just one year later, they struck again. A maidservant was told to quietly conduct the pursuivants to the master's bedroom. The quick-witted girl stood her ground and called loudly up the stairs, giving Bray and Blount a precious warning. They got away – just. Barefoot and with no clothes other than their breeches and Blount's cassock, they gathered their books, vestments, a little wine and a small loaf. Then, they made for their hide. This particular hide was off the small courtyard to the east of the old hall range, where a pivoting stone slab covered a cavity low in a thick stone wall. Mrs Darrell and her two children (William and Rose) were confined to a room over the gatehouse. For ten days, the fugitives were trapped.

Towards the end of the period, the family were permitted to move around. Mrs Darrell took the opportunity to cross the courtyard and glance towards the hide. To her horror, she noticed that a tassel from a vestment girdle was protruding from the stone slab! She stooped down, cut it and said, 'pull in the string', which the fugitives did. Unfortunately, she was under observation and was immediately asked whom she was speaking to and to what string she was referring (a hasty excuse about asking someone to pull the latch string of a nearby door that had been shut against her did not wash). Searchers were summoned, and they began beating the walls with mattocks. A mason employed by the pursuivants noticed that a stone in the turret was not original, so they set to work there. Soon, the hinges of the door began to give way and Bray and Blount had to lean against it with their backs. They could hear the searcher's every word and, in the growing dark, the light of their candles could be seen through the cracks.

It began to rain heavily. Soon, water began spilling over the gutters and on to the searcher's heads. Cold, wet and sapped of their fanatical zeal, a decision was made to abandon the search until the next morning. After all, they reasoned, even if the fugitives were hidden behind the wall, they were surrounded by icy moat water. The searchers retired to the comfort of the hall and its roaring fire – neglecting, it seems, to post sentries by the suspect stone.

This was a mistake. The lucky fugitives emerged from their hide into the rain-lashed night. They crossed the courtyard and scaled two 3m walls to reach a ruined tower at the eastern corner of the moat. The moat, however, was some 25m wide at this point and unfordable. What is more, the water was covered with a thin sheet of ice and timber piles lay just below the surface (rediscovered in 1863). Still, Blount removed his cassock and, from a height of 5m, leapt over them. Bray could not swim, so he was going to leap in after Blount so the priest could help him across. However, weak with hunger and immersed in freezing water, Blount used what little strength he had to reach the other side. Clambering to safety he called back to Bray, 'I am so weak ... If I should come back to fetch you, we should both be drowned.'

So instead, Blount directed Bray to the stables on the outer island, beyond the gatehouse. Behind the stables the moat was shallow and he could wade across, concealed beneath trees. Once safely over, he was to go to the home of one of Scotney's former Catholic servants, just under 1km away.

Bray was faced with a problem. To reach his fording point, he had to cross the causeway via the gatehouse. Undeterred, he tucked his cassock into his breeches and burst into the hall, shouting, 'My master has heard a noise in the stable, and says he thinks someone is stealing his horses, and you all sit drinking here and nobody looks to his horses!'

Startled and not considering who this man was, the searchers rushed through the causeway gatehouse and made for the stables. Bray kept with them – but not for long.

Finding everything in order in the stables, the company began asking one another who the alarm raiser was and where he had gone. One of them said he saw a man in a strange habit, and heard someone plunge into the moat. Realising it must have been a priest, and believing him drowned, the moat was dragged – giving Bray time to escape.

Meanwhile, Bray had stumbled upon Father Blount (it seems he lost his bearings and ended up back at the castle). Together, they made for the safe house where they were fed, clothed and their sore and bloodied feet washed. That very night the exhausted pair put a further 23km between themselves and Scotney Castle – and it is lucky they did. At first light the hide was found. Bloodhounds were immediately put to the scent but, by then, it was too late.

There is a final twist. Whilst the search was underway, a Protestant plough-boy arrived at the house. Terrified by the sight of the searchers, he hid in the hay. Just as they were dragging the moat, the hungry boy went foraging for meat and was spotted. 'The Priest! The Priest!' When Mr Darrell was accused of priest harbouring, he was able to use this to his advantage. He claimed the charge was a lie, a trumped-up case inspired by the boy's capture. Since no priest was found, the case was dropped.

Scotney remained with the Darrell family for 350 years, until it was purchased by Edward Hussey in 1778. The 'new' castle was built on higher ground by his grandson, also named Edward, to designs by Anthony Salvin. It boasts numerous interesting features, including a gib door in the library, cunningly disguised as a bookcase.

Lamberhurst, Tunbridge Wells TN3 8JN; National Trust, open all year.

11. ABDICATION HOUSE, RESTORATION HOUSE AND EASTGATE HOUSE KENT

Rochester possesses considerable antiquarian interest and was the haunt of nineteenth-century novelist Charles Dickens.

A plaque at Abdication House reads, 'King James II of England and VII of Scotland stayed at this house as the guest of Sir Richard Head before embarking for France on the 23rd December 1688 when he finally left England.'

England's last Roman Catholic sovereign was deposed in the Glorious Revolution of 1688–89 and replaced by the joint monarchy of his Protestant daughter, Mary, and her Dutch husband, William of Orange. The seventeenth-century town house retains original panelling and had a secret route from

Restoration House by Kent artist Marion Smith.

the attic, now long forgotten. Just as well, really. Today it is a branch of Lloyds TSB!

Restoration House is associated with a happier event, since this was the first house that Charles II slept in following his return from exile in France. Grade I listed and architecturally complex, it likely began as two late medieval buildings that were amalgamated during the sixteenth and seventeenth centuries to create a mansion house. Then known as Crow Lane House, the picturesque, red-brick building was occupied by a Nicholas Morgan during the late sixteenth century and in 1607 passed to Henry Clerke (*c.* 1580–1652), twice MP for Rochester and a staunch Royalist. He developed the house considerably, *perhaps* creating a Civil War-era hiding place cum bolt hole.

From the gardens a small, semicircular waste exit hole is visible on right hand side of the house on the lower ground floor, and in line with this are two circular windows corresponding to the floors above. This was a garderobe (latrine) block and the windows provided ventilation for the closets on each floor. If hides were ever required, the closet doorways could easily be blocked and secret entrances made. Granville Squires thought he had found evidence for such a conversion and speculated that the windows above must have been covered by ivy, making them difficult to spot.

The entrances on the lower ground floor (from the old kitchen) and from the King's Bedchamber were indeed blocked, but probably for practical reasons. In a cupboard between the two aforementioned floors, Squires saw a trapdoor in the top of it (apparently leading to the garrets) and thought there would have been another leading to the chamber adjoining the exit hole, below. Any trapdoors are long gone, and the cupboard is today presented as a survival garderobe, later divided for various (practical) reasons.

Exterior and interior views of the garderobe shaft at Restoration House.

The house also captured Charles Dickens' imagination. The great writer grew up in nearby Chatham, so he knew Rochester well. At the age of 9 his father told him that if he worked hard, he would one day own a house like Gad's Hill Place, an eighteenth-century red-brick mansion in Higham. Afterwards, Dickens visited frequently, gazing at his future home and imagining a successful future. His father's prediction came to pass – he moved into Gad's Hill Place in 1857. Dickens' study, which he furnished with a mock bookcase door, has been preserved. He wrote some of his greatest works in a miniature Swiss chalet in the garden and built a tunnel under the highway to reach it. The chalet has been moved, but the tunnel remains.

Many of Rochester's buildings are recognisable in Dickens' books, especially *Great Expectations*, which is set in and around the city. According to Dickens' biographer John Forster, aspects of Restoration House were used for the description of Miss Havisham's Satis House:

> Within a quarter of an hour we came to Miss Havisham's House, which was of old brick and dismal, and had a great many iron bars to it ... There was a court-yard in front, and that was barred; so we had to wait, after ringing the bell, until someone should come to open it ... We went into the house by a side-door – the great front entrance had two chains across it outside – and the first thing I noticed was that the passages were all dark, and that she had left a candle burning there. She took it up, and we went through more passages and up a staircase and still it was all dark, and only the candle lighted us.

Eastgate House is a beautiful Elizabethan townhouse built about 1590–91 for Sir Peter Buck, Clerk of the Cheque at Chatham Dockyard. It featured as 'Westgate' in Dickens' novel *Pickwick Papers* and as 'the Nun's House' in *The Mystery of Edwin Droode*. In Dickens' time it was used as a boarding school for young ladies, and his beautiful Swiss chalet now stands in its gardens. On the afternoon of the day he died, Dickens wrote the final pages of *The Mystery of Edwin Droode* in the upper room.

Fitting, then, that mystery surrounds Eastgate House. According to tradition, it had a hiding place and there was a secret tunnel hereabouts.

Restoration House: 17–19 Crow Lane, Rochester ME1 1RF; private house open to the public, open part year.

Gad's Hill Place: Gravesend Road, Higham ME3 7PA; now a school, tours on special open days.

Eastgate House: High Street; Rochester ME1 1EW; museum, open all year.

12. Mapledurham House Oxfordshire

Since Mapledurham is one of Oxfordshire's largest Elizabethan houses, expectations will be high. It will not disappoint. This gorgeous mansion superseded an older, adjacent manor house called Mapledurham Gurney. Located next to the River Thames, the grounds of the present house are graced by the only working flour mill in the Thames Valley. Little wonder Mapledurham was the model for Toad Hall in Kenneth Graeme's children's classic, *The Wind in the Willows*.

Built to an H-plan in red brick and with two storeys and an attic, Mapledurham was begun around 1588 by Sir Michael Blount and completed by his son, Sir Richard (1564–1628).

From 1590 to 1595, Sir Michael was Lieutenant of the Tower of London. He was so moved by the plight of two men in his charge – the Jesuit missionary Father Robert Southwell (1561–95) and Philip Howard, 20th Earl of Arundel (1557–95) – that he became a Catholic convert. In 1592, Southwell was arrested at Uxendon Hall,[45] Harrow, after six years of zealous missionary work, 'hearing confessions and other priestly duties, hemmed in by daily perils, never safe for a moment'. He was taken to the Westminster home of the queen's chief priest hunter, a sadistic rapist called Richard Topcliffe (1531–1604). Here he was manacled by the wrists in Topcliffe's private torture chamber. Topcliffe felt able to act with impunity, was clearly disturbed and openly boasted about the instruments of torture he had assembled at his house. However, after failing to extract any intelligence, he moved the priest to the Gatehouse Prison adjoining Westminster Abbey. Here he spent weeks festering in his own filth; crawling with lice and maggots.

Alarmed by the conditions in which his son was being kept, Southwell's father begged the queen to treat him like the gentleman he was. She agreed, and he was allowed provisions, clothing and a Bible. He was then taken to the Tower where he was kept in solitary confinement and tortured over three years.

In 1595, Southwell was convicted on charges of treason and dragged on a sled to Tyburn (close to Marble Arch in present-day London). As he stood in the cart below the gibbet, hands bound, he made the sign of the cross as best he could. He began reciting a Bible passage from *Romans* XIV and made other statements, confessing he was a Jesuit and praying for queen and country. As the cart was drawn away, he commended his soul to God.

After being hung for a short time, he again attempted the sign of the cross. According to the sentence, Southwell was to be taken down alive and disembowelled. However, to hasten his passing Lord Mountjoy (Charles Blount) and others tugged at the priest's legs. At the end of the grizzly spectacle, Southwell's head was held aloft. There were none of the usual shouts of 'Traitor!'

Philip Howard suffered an equally tragic fate. As a recusant, and as second cousin (once removed) to the queen, he was at great risk. In 1585 he was betrayed by a servant and committed to the Tower. In constant fear of execution,

Howard's only comfort was his dog, through which messages of support and encouragement were sent between prisoners (most notably Southwell). Whilst in his cell he scratched the following words on to the wall, '*Quanto plus afflictiones pro Christo in hoc saeculo, tanto plus gloriae cum Christo in futuro*' ('The more afflictions we endure for Christ in this world, the more glory we shall obtain in the next').

He spent ten years in the Tower, and eventually became unwell. As he lay dying he petitioned the queen to see his wife and son (born after his imprisonment). She responded thus, 'If he will but once attend the Protestant service, he shall not only see his wife and children, but be restored to his honours and estates with every mark of my royal favour.'

To this, Howard replied, 'Tell Her Majesty, if my religion be the cause for which I suffer, sorry I am that I have but one life to lose.'

Howard never saw his wife and son. He died alone in the Tower on Sunday, 19 October 1595.

Sir Michael's son, Sir Richard, was almost certainly a Catholic but it seems he professed ambivalence and kept a low profile. However, Sir Richard's wife, Cecily (Baker), and his extravagant Royalist son, Sir Charles, were outright recusants. The house was besieged and sacked by Roundheads under the Earl of Essex in 1643 and, one year later, Sir Charles died when a Royalist sentry accidently shot him.

Mapledurham's isolated, riverside location made secrecy, stealthy travel and escape much easier. A high gable overlooking the river is studded with oyster shells, perhaps a covert sign that this was a safe refuge for Catholics. And safe it was – for there were abundant priest holes here. The trapdoors of two of Mapledurham's hides had rare wooden spring bolts operated via string, like those at nearby Ufton Court, and Hodgetts attributes them to the same builder (probably Nicholas Owen).

They can be found in a first-floor room. One of them – the smaller of the two – is under a cupboard floor, while the other is under a garderobe. It measures 2m by 1.2m, is 1m deep and has a well-preserved trapdoor. A further hide was discovered in 2002. It is located in another upper bedroom, beneath a sliding hearth.

Reading RG4 7TR; private house and estate, hosts various events and group tours by appointment.

13. Chastleton House Oxfordshire

〰〰

A romantic, Civil War-era tale is associated with a secret hiding place here. Now in the hands of the National Trust, this fine Jacobean country house has remained much the same for four centuries. It was built between 1607 and 1612 by prosperous clothier Walter Jones, though at one point the estate was owned by the Gunpowder Plot instigator, Robert Catesby. Since the Jones' were not recusants, Chastleton's hide probably relates to the Civil War period.

Now a panelled dressing room, it is located over the porch and was masked by a dummy row of lights in a twelve-light window. The porch ceiling has been lowered, and begins at the second transom up. Behind the dummy row of lights (the top row) there is a blank wall, behind which is the former hide.

Following defeat at the Battle of Worcester, Captain Arthur Jones (a Cavalier member of the family) fled back to the house. He was one step ahead of a group of Roundheads, and on reaching the house, made straight for the hide. His wife challenged his pursuers in the hall and, on hearing who they were after, coolly offered to conduct them around the house.

Upon reaching the room adjacent to the hide, a member of the party became suspicious and the Roundheads refused to leave that night. Wisely, Mrs Jones put up no resistance. Instead she plied the men with hearty food and large quantities of strong beer.

The men soon fell into a deep, alcohol-induced sleep and Mrs Jones felt confident enough to call her husband. By the time the Roundheads awoke, Captain Jones was, of course, long gone.

Moreton-in-Marsh GL56 0SU; National Trust, open part year.

14. Ham House Surrey

〰〰

Located on the River Thames, this exquisite residence was built in 1610 by Sir Thomas Vavasour, Knight Marshall to James I. It later came into the possession of Elizabeth Murray, Countess of Dysart (1626–98) after she inherited the estate from her father, William Murray, 1st Earl of Dysart (c. 1600–53). Murray was a childhood whipping boy, and later an advisor to Charles II. He added much to the house: the Great Staircase, the Long Gallery, the Hall Gallery and the North Drawing Room, but his daughter, a supporter of the future Charles II in his exile (and member of the Sealed Knot society) was not satisfied.

With her second husband, John Maitland, Duke of Lauderdale (1616–82) she added even greater splendour: Ham House today is one of the nation's greatest surviving seventeenth-century houses.

In *Secret Chambers and Hiding Places*, Allan Fea wrote of a secret staircase, said to have been used by James II after he had been sent here prior to his flight from Britain. Indeed, secret passageways and hidden stairs abound. They are of a fairly recent type, designed to keep domestic servants out of the sight of the haughty, upper-class owners.

Ham Street, Richmond-upon-Thames TW10 7RS; National Trust, open part year.

15. Byfleet Manor Surrey

Architectural historian Nikolaus Pevsner called Byfleet one of England's most attractive, late seventeenth-century houses, 'a great surprise, with its small scale formality and mellow red brick'. Little wonder it doubles as Dowager Violet's house in the hugely popular television drama *Downton Abbey*.

Like many historic properties Byfleet is a hybrid, the present house of 1686 incorporating puzzling details from earlier periods. Its history is impressive. There was a royal hunting lodge here and, in the early fourteenth century, Edward II made a present of it to his unpopular favourite, Piers Gaveston

Byfleet Manor in the snow. The property doubles as Dowager Violet's house in *Downton Abbey*.

(*c.* 1284–1312). After reverting to the Crown the manor passed through various royal hands, and was traditionally granted by kings of England to their eldest sons. Eventually, it passed from James I to Henry, Prince of Wales (1594–1612) and after his son's death to his consort, Anne of Denmark (thought by some to have secretly converted to Roman Catholicism). It was she who rebuilt the manor house in a grand, palatial style, possibly under the guidance of Inigo Jones. She died in 1619, just prior to its completion. It was left to the subsequent tenant, Sir James Fullerton (*c.* 1563–1631) to complete the house. In 1675, Byfleet was leased to the Earl of St Albans and sublet to a William

This old drain was long belived to be a subterranean passage.

Sutton. Sutton petitioned Charles II for permission to rebuild the property on the grounds that it was in a ruinous condition. Authorisation for the works was signed by Sir Christopher Wren on behalf of the king (it is not known whether Wren took part in the endeavour). In 1686, Sutton rebuilt Byfleet Manor House using materials from the old palace and Pevsner thought he had 'made a very sober, elegant job of it'.

There are several curiosities. Visitors will be interested in the unexplored tunnel in the garden, long rumoured to be a secret route to the ruins of Newark Abbey. Its purpose, however, is no mystery, 'The ancient drain in the garden is interesting. It probably belonged to the royal hunting lodge, and was long believed to be a subterranean passage on account of its size.'[46]

At present, it is not known whether the drain is associated with the old hunting lodge or, as seems more likely, Queen Anne's palace.

Venturing into Byfleet's cellar, four wooden steps ascend to a wall. It is impossible to determine what, if anything, lies behind it. More mysterious still is the room discovered between floors in 2013. Some 2m square, it has a bricked-up window and papered walls (indicating signs of use). Given the late date of the house, it is almost certainly not a priest hole. Theories about its purpose range from safe room to secret love nest.

West Byfleet KT14 7RS; private house available for special occasions and events by arrangement.

16. REIGATE CASTLE SURREY

It is possible to join tours of the extraordinary, finely worked caverns beneath Reigate Castle. The castle itself had eleventh-century origins, beginning as an earthwork ring-motte and bailey fortress, later replaced by a substantial stone castle. Today, all that remains are the caverns.

The Baron's Cave (the collective name for the passages) was imagined to be a secret meeting place for medieval barons on their way to sign Magna Carta. Located under the western inner closure, there is an entrance under a curious stone pyramid in the middle of the castle site, and another in the western ditch. The caverns were first mentioned in William Camden's *Britannia*, published in 1586, though are certainly much older. He saw, 'an extraordinary passage with a vaulted roof hewn with great labour out of the soft stone'.

Sand was extensively mined in these parts, but parts of the Baron's Cave exhibit fine workmanship and its origins are unclear. Theories abound, but the most likely explanation is that the longest of the passages began as a sally port, and that over time dry cellars and store houses were added.

Reigate RH2 9QT; Wealden Cave & Mine Society (WCMS) conduct tours of Baron's Cave, as well as other caves off Tunnel Road. Public open days also.

17. ROYAL PAVILION SUSSEX

This extravagant building was begun in 1787 as a seaside retreat for George, Prince of Wales (1762–1830). Built in the Indo-Saracenic style and reminiscent of the Taj Mahal, the building has long been associated with secret tunnels. At least one exists, located under the pavilion gardens. Constructed in 1821, the 60m passage allowed the unpopular prince to cross the estate in secret as he made his way from the house to the stables.

Pavilion Buildings, Brighton BN1 1EE UK; museum, open all year.

18. Michelham Priory Sussex

◇◇◇

Michelham Priory occupies one of the most beautiful sites in Sussex and boasts England's longest water-filled moat. Founded by Gilbert de l'Aigle in 1229, this former Augustinian priory sits on a partial island in the River Cuckmere (Michelham is said to mean 'hemmed in piece of land'). Following the Dissolution of the Monasteries, part of the old priory was incorporated into the wonderful Elizabethan House built by Herbert Pelham in about 1595. In 1601, the house was sold to Queen Elizabeth's cousin Thomas Sackville, Lord of Buckhurst (1536–1608) and remained in that family for three centuries. It was gifted to its present owners by the Sussex Archaeological Society in 1959.

Of note here are the curious features behind the panelling next to the main staircase, much damaged by a fire in 1927 and subsequently replaced. A cupboard on the ground floor allows entry into a space with a series of ladders and platforms. On the first floor there is a moveable panel that may have been a spyhole. The feature continues up to the second floor, terminating at a cupboard whose door is part of the panelling. Is it a reproduction of a genuine secret hiding place, or an entirely recent folly?

Upper Dicker, Hailsham BN27 3QS; open part year.

Above and right: spot the difference. Curious features are concealed behind the panelling next to the main staircase. The cupboard in the picture allows entry into a space with a series of ladders and platforms.

Left: Michelham Priory.

Arundel Castle was founded on Christmas Day 1067 when William the Conqueror conferred the earldom and castle on the Norman knight, Roger de Montgomery (*c*.1030–94). The title was handed down to the d'Albini, the Fitzalan and finally, in 1580, to their heirs the Howards, dukes of Norfolk.

Twice besieged during the Civil War, by the time Horace Walpole visited in 1749 Arundel was largely ruinous and barely habitable. Fortunately, it survived and today the medieval castle incorporates the largest inhabited Victorian Gothic Revival house in England.

Built in around 1138, the fine shell keep has 3m thick walls and contains a thirteenth-century vaulted cellar. A subterraneous sally port from the barbican/gatehouse leads to a dry ditch at the foot of the Norman motte mound.

There is little to support a tradition of a secret passageway that ran from the castle towards Amberley. However, the Howards were one of England's foremost recusant families and, as England's chief Catholic house, Arundel likely contained secret hiding places. Granville Squires thought he had found one under the Small Drawing Room (now the duke's sitting room): 'a trap-door, covered by a carpet, and below it is a hiding place, not very large, concealed by a false wall or buttress in the cellar'.

The Howards of Arundel Castle were one of England's foremost recusant families.

The Chapel at Arundel Castle.

The Drawing Room, Arundel Castle. Historian Granville Squires noted a carpet-covered trapdoor in the Small Drawing Room.

Connected to the lavishly furnished Drawing Room, the Small or Ante Drawing Room occupies a tower built by the eccentric 11th Duke of Norfolk, Charles Howard (1746–1815). Below it is a Norman undercroft – a type of cellar or storage room. According to Dr John Martin Robinson, librarian to the Duke of Norfolk, a modern trapdoor merely gives access to the lower part of the tower and the false wall or buttress referred to by Squires is, in fact, a brick-supporting wall built in around 1790.

Secret chambers or not, this stately castle is awash with antiquities. The 11th Duke's library is fitted out in Honduran mahogany and its treasures include a replica Viking horn and some 10,000 books, many of which relate to the history of the Catholic religion. Notably, there are fifty-eight volumes of seventeenth-century pamphlets on the Catholic controversy of the reign of James II.

A collection of former personal possessions of Mary, Queen of Scots are on show in the Dining Room. They include a cross and rosary beads of gold and enamel that she carried to her own execution at Fotheringhay Castle, a wooden pomander of rosary beads (said to have a relic of the true cross) and an exquisite necklace of River Tay pearls, separated by gold fleurs-de-lis.

Arundel BN18 9AB; private castle open to visitors part year.

20. CHICHESTER CATHEDRAL SUSSEX

◇◇

Founded in 1075, Chichester Cathedral contains many antiquities. Its rich and varied architecture is complemented by medieval misericords and artfully carved tombs. There is even a Roman mosaic floor. However, of particular interest is a curiously concealed room known as Lollard's Prison.

Approached via a sliding panel in the old consistory room (court room) over the south porch, a concealed door leads to a 4.6m by 3.7m room in which fifteenth-century heretics were confined.

Or so it is said. The prison story does not quite tally with the facts – after all, it would hardly be necessary to conceal a prison door. In reality, this was the old treasury – a room for important documents or valuables. It is now the Song School, the space having been set aside for the Cathedral Choir to meet for lessons and to practice. Although normally closed to the public, visitors can see the room on a behind-the-scenes tour.

Chichester PO19 1RP; open daily with free entry. Free guided tours Monday to Saturday. All are welcome.

Opposite: Chichester Cathedral.

21. GREAT CHALFIELD WILTSHIRE

Ever had a feeling you were being watched? At Great Chalfield, you would be right. The walls have eyes!

Set in a pretty hamlet amidst woods and farmland, this beautiful, atmospheric manor house was built between 1467 and 1480 by wealthy clothier Thomas Tropenell. It was a time of turmoil, and Great Chalfield was suitably defended by a moat and a high outer wall with semicircular bastions (of which little survives).

The house appears Tudor and much of the entrance front (including the oak door) is original. However, its present appearance is largely the result of a twentieth-century restoration by Sir Harold Drakespear for Major Robert Fuller. Major Fuller furnished Great Chalfield with period tapestries and fine eastern rugs.

Of special interest are some curious squints (wall openings) of a rare design through which the lord, when he retired, could observe what was going on. The squints at Great Chalfield take the form of three hollow stone masks in the great hall: a laughing face in the wall above the minstrel's gallery and two at the opposite end (a bishop with a mitre and a king with ass's ears). In addition, visitors coming through the porch could be assessed through a squint from the dining room.

Near Melksham SN12 8NH; National Trust, limited opening part year (house by guided tour only).

22. THE TOWER OF LONDON

Her Majesty's Royal Palace and Fortress – The Tower of London – needs little by way of introduction. It has played an important role in the history of the English nation ever since William the Conqueror built his White Tower in 1078.

Hundreds were tortured and died here, mainly during the religious upheavals of the sixteenth and seventeenth centuries. The Jesuit priest John Gerard was captured and tortured in the Tower in April 1597. He wrote vividly of his suffering:[47]

> We went to the torture room in a kind of procession, the attendants walking ahead with lighted candles.
> The chamber was underground and dark, particularly near the entrance. It was a vast place and every device and instrument of human torture was there. They pointed out some of them to me and said I would try them all. Then he asked me again whether I would confess.
> 'I cannot,' I said.

I fell on my knees for a moment's prayer. Then they took me to a big upright pillar, one of the wooden posts which held the roof of this huge underground chamber. Driven into the top of it were iron staples for supporting heavy weights. Then they put my wrists into iron gauntlets and ordered me to climb two or three wicker steps. My arms were then lifted up and an iron bar was passed through the rings of one gauntlet, then through the staple and rings to the second gauntlet. This done, they fastened the bar with a pin to prevent it from slipping, and then, removing the wicker steps one by one from under my feet, they left me hanging by my hands and arms fastened above my head. The tips of my toes, however, still touched the ground, and they had to dig the earth away from under them. They had hung me up from the highest staple in the pillar and could not raise me any higher, without driving in another staple.

Hanging like this I began to pray. The gentlemen standing around me asked me whether I was willing to confess now.

'I cannot and I will not,' I answered.

But I could hardly utter the words; such a gripping pain came over me. It was worst in my chest and belly, my hands and arms. All the blood in my body seemed to rush up into my arms and hands and I thought that blood was oozing from the ends of my fingers and the pores of my skin. But it was only a sensation caused by my flesh swelling above the irons holding them.

The pain was so intense that I thought I could not possibly endure it, and added to it, I had an interior temptation. Yet I did not feel any inclination or wish to give them the information they wanted.

... A little later they took me down. My legs and feet were not damaged, but it was a great effort to stand upright.

A subtler form of torture required the use of a chamber known as 'Little Ease'. Barely 1.2m square, it was impossible for the prisoner to find a comfortable position (Jesuit priest Edmund Campion was kept in it for four days). Its exact location has long been a matter for speculation.

Naturally, many legends have become attached to the Tower. In particular, the grim fortress is said to have innumerable ghosts and has long been supposed to have a labyrinth of secret passageways. There was excitement when a vaulted underground passage of 'Cimmerian depths' that 'reeked with the oozing damp of centuries' was discovered around the turn of the twentieth century. It began in a beehive-shaped dungeon under the south-west corner of the White Tower, and ran to the moat near the Wakefield Tower. It was, of course, a main drain. However, given that the aforementioned dungeon was connected to a drain, it is possible this was the 'dungeon amongst the ratts', a fabled hell-hole described as a sort of cave with no light, some 6m deep, which at high tide became infested with rats seeking shelter.

Tower Hill EC3N 4AB; Historic Royal Palaces, open all year.

23. ELTHAM PALACE INNER LONDON

◇◇

Eltham developed as a moated medieval palace in the fourteenth century and was transformed in the 1930s into an ostentatious private house. Little of the ancient palace remains, other than the moated enclosure, the moat bridge, the fifteenth-century Great Hall, the foundations of various buildings – and an intricate network of subterranean tunnels.

The dank tunnels are high, wide and brick-vaulted. Two lead to obvious arches at the moat side. Another range is accessed via a short, vertical brick shaft. The shaft leads to a large tunnel parallel to the southern side of a dry part of the moat, with short passages and chambers leading off it to the north. It terminates at a vertical shaft up to a grill near the south bridge. Here a branch goes down under the moat, terminating at a short flight of steps into a field.

Reputed to be 'escape tunnels' (or secret passageways for Henry VIII to travel incognito), they are in fact drains that were connected to the palace kitchens and garderobes via stairs and chutes. Drains such as this were typical arrangements in high-status buildings – and are the source of many a tall tale!

Court Yard, Greenwich SE9 5QE; English Heritage, limited opening part year (Sundays in winter).

EAST ANGLIA

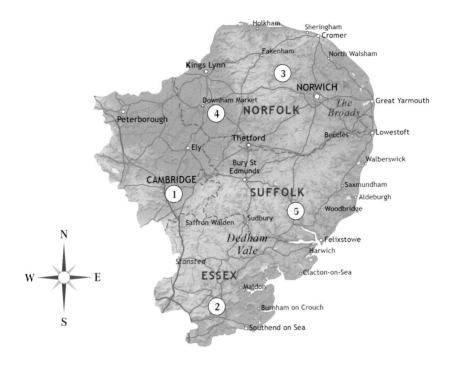

From the great university city of Cambridge to the bittern-haunted broads, East Anglia is wonderfully distinctive. Its hidden heritage will captivate, enchant and delight.

1. MADINGLEY HALL CAMBRIDGESHIRE

This fine, red-brick Tudor mansion was probably built for the English judge Sir John Hynde between 1543 and 1547. Early survivals include the range between the matching turrets containing the ground-floor hall and the chamber above, parts of the hall fireplace and a false hammer-beam roof.

The Hyndes owned Madingley until 1647 when Jane, the sole heiress, married Sir John Cotton, Baronet of Landwade (d. 1689). The Hynde-Cottons were Royalists and Sir John Hynde-Cotton, 3rd Baronet (*c*.1688–1752) was a notorious Jacobite. Madingley remained the family's seat until 1858. In 1860, the hall was let by the then owner, Lady King, as a residence for Edward, Prince of Wales, while he was studying at Cambridge. In 1948 it was bought by University of Cambridge and remains in their possession to the present day.

Madingley has, or had, several secret hiding places. One traditional location in a room on the first floor is little more than an unusual corner. Another is in a gable, next to a room reminiscent of those used as secret chapels. During his investigations, priest-hole hunter Granville Squires received a letter from a Rev. Jocelyn James Antrobus informing him that he was given the location of the secret hiding places by his 88-year-old great aunt (who had lived at the hall until it was sold out of their family in 1871). Unfortunately, he did not make notes and the details were forgotten!

In June 1647, Cromwell had Charles I confined to the principal room on the upper floor of Childerley Hall,[48] some 5km away. According to tradition, the king slipped away to Madingley Hall disguised in a peasant's smock, and since the family were staunch Royalists, was promptly hidden in a roof hide.

The hiding place could not have been very secret since he was quickly found and taken back to Childerley. It is said the story was hushed up since both the king and Parliament wanted to give the impression he was a willing captive, rather than under house arrest.

Madingley, Cambridge CB23 8AQ; University of Cambridge, events, conferences and accommodation. Tours may be available locally.

2. INGATESTONE HALL ESSEX

The Petre family have always adhered to the old faith, and soon after the Dissolution of the Monasteries, Sir William Petre built a mansion on the hallowed site of Barking Abbey. Unlike later generations of the family, Sir William must have kept a low profile when it came to religion. He served as Secretary of State to four Tudor monarchs: Henry VIII, Edward VI, Mary I and Elizabeth I. He had found the old abbey steward's house 'scarce mete for a fermor to dwell on' so he demolished it and built a superb four-sided, red-brick mansion around a central courtyard. In fact it was fit for a queen and in 1561 Elizabeth I spent several nights here.

Ingatestone remains the seat of the Petre family who today occupy the south wing. Though much modified and somewhat reduced over the centuries, the house has an ancient atmosphere and boasts an abundance of Tudor portraits, tapestries and carved oak panelling (Mary Elizabeth Braddon's *Lady Audley's Secret* is set in and around the hall, and was inspired by a stay here).

The Petre family's motto '*Sans Dieu Rien*' ('Without God, Nothing') appears on a centuries-old clock tower above the half-timbered gatehouse. Priests were welcome here, including the Roman Catholic martyr, John Payne. Payne was born in 1532 and brought up as a Protestant – but at some point he converted to Roman Catholicism, trained in Douai, France, and in 1576 was ordained as a priest.

After Sir William Petre's death in 1572, Payne for the most part resided at Ingatestone with Lady Petre, ministering not only to the household, but to the local Catholic community.

In 1581 Payne was betrayed by George 'Judas' Elliot, a notable priest catcher and confidence trickster. Payne was arrested at Ingatestone, taken to the Tower of London and twice tortured on a rack (ostensibly accused of plotting to murder Queen Elizabeth and install Mary, Queen of Scots on the throne). The verdict was a forgone conclusion. In April 1582, Payne was hung, drawn and quartered at Chelmsford.

Two possible priest holes are pointed out today, both in the south range. One is on the ground floor of a 4.3m-wide projecting stair tower, across which a false wall was built 60cm from the end to create a secret chamber. The sole entrance is a modern trapdoor in the floorboards above. Upon discovery, the chamber was found to contain an ancient storage chest and there was a clay candle holder stuck on the wall. On the floor was a layer of sand in which bird bones were found, the remains of a meal. In the 1930s a smaller priest hole was found in the richly panelled old study, behind the Stone Hall chimney stack.

Hall Lane, Ingatestone CM4 9NR; private house open to the public, limited seasonal opening.

3. Elsing Hall Norfolk

◇◇

Set amidst beautiful gardens, Elsing Hall is a quintessentially English moated manor house. Dating to the mid-fifteenth century and probably built for John Hastings (1438−77), a mid-nineteenth-century discovery hints that there is more to the hall than is generally known.

A hidden stairwell was discovered during alterations overseen by the architect Thomas Jeckyll (1827−81). The local rector wrote the following description of the discovery, dated 29 April 1876:

> At Elsing Hall, between the grand hall and the withdrawing-room, in the thick of the wall is a well, evidently the well of a staircase leading downwards. The curious part of this is that the opening was in the side of the room; it was therefore no cellar, but most probably a place of concealment. The plastered wall of the well against the hall was broken into during the repairs some twenty years ago, and then I saw it.[49]

The rector appears to be referring to a spiral stair that Jeckyll discovered between the former solar and a blocked cellar below the parlour (now the library). In his *Greater Medieval Houses of England and Wales*, Anthony Emery says that a recent owner found the remains of the aforementioned stair near the upper doorway of the former solar, concealed behind eighteenth-century panelling.

So the rector was mistaken in his belief that the stairwell led to a hide. However, a concealed stair to a blocked cellar is a satisfying alternative!

Elsing, Dereham, NR20 3DX; private house not generally open to the public, garden open to groups of twenty or more by prior arrangement and visits include an introductory talk giving the history of the hall. Occasionally hosts functions in the gardens.

4. OXBURGH HALL NORFOLK

◇◇

Who could forget their first sight of Oxburgh Hall? Built of mellow red brick, this majestic, moat-enclosed mansion consists of four domestic ranges around a courtyard. A little off-centre in the north front, the boldly projecting fifteenth-century gatehouse is the least altered part of the house. It was designed to provide lodgings for distinguished visitors, and is flanked on either side by an octagonal tower, each one machicolated, embattled and rising to over 20m above the causeway of the bridge. Despite these 'fortifications', Oxburgh was built to impress and was never a stronghold.

Impress it does, both outside and in. In addition, the ancestral home of the staunchly Catholic Bedingfields (who still occupy part of the house) has a fine and famous priest hole.

After serving both Edward IV and Henry VII during the Wars of the Roses, Sir Edmund Bedingfield (1443–96) was a rising courtier. He inherited Oxburgh in 1476 and a licence to crenellate, dated 3 July 1482, is preserved here. By that date work on the house was already underway, since the licence includes a pardon for constructing fortifications without permission. In 1487, Sir Edmund was made a knight banneret.

The Bedingfields again found royal favour during the brief reign of Mary I (r. 1553–58). In July 1553, Sir Edmund's grandson, Sir Henry Bedingfield (1509–83) had been among the first to rally to Mary in opposition to the rival claim of Lady Jane Grey. He was appointed to the Privy Council and helped to suppress Wyatt's Rebellion of 1554 against Queen Mary's decision to marry Phillip II of Spain. From 1554–55, Sir Henry was charged with guarding Princess Elizabeth at the Tower of London, and then at the Royal Manor of Woodstock, Oxfordshire (in effect, she was under house arrest). Though stern and controlling, he treated his charge with honour and respect – and Sir Henry's close supervision protected Elizabeth from assassins.

After Elizabeth's accession in 1558, Bedingfield presented himself at court with apologies for his previous conduct. The queen, 'with a nipping word', remarked, 'If we have any prisoner who we would have sharply and straitly

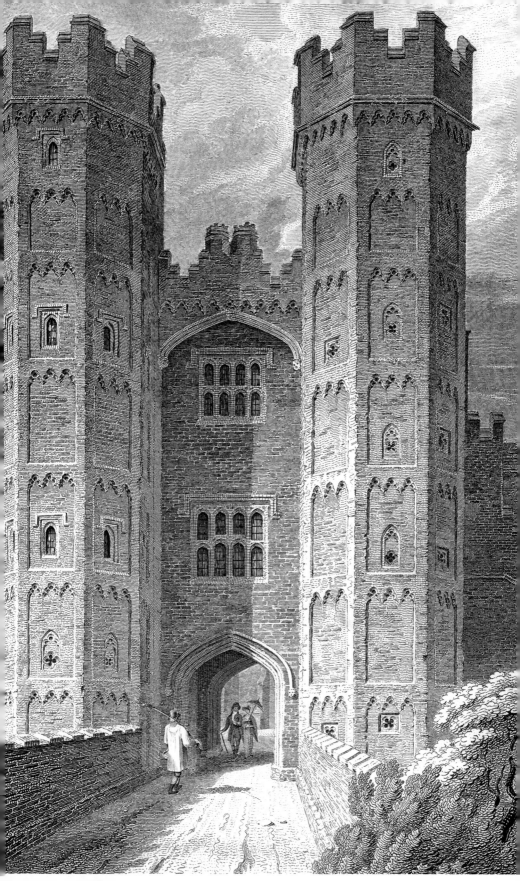

kept, we will send for you.' Sir Henry slunk back to Oxburgh. However, as a prominent recusant, the quiet life proved elusive.

The fugitive priest John Gerard almost certainly visited Oxburgh and he likely received a warm welcome. Sir Henry refused to obey the Act of Uniformity (1559) and was required to pay heavy fines for non-attendance of the parish church. His servants were dismissed (one of whom was said to be a priest in disguise), and his house was searched repeatedly.

No wonder they did not find anything. Rediscovered in the late eighteenth century and sometimes referred to as the 'dungeon', Oxburgh's priest hole was solid, secure and soundproof. Unusually, visitors may explore it.

Over the arch of the gatehouse on the first floor there is a large vaulted apartment called the King's Room (after Henry VII, said to have slept here in 1487). Crossing the room, one enters an octagonal vaulted closet via an arched doorway in the east turret of the gatehouse and from there a narrow, elbowed passage rising five steps leads to a small brick-vaulted room with a tiled floor in the rectangular garderobe (latrine) turret. In one corner of this room there is an arched recess (for the latrine), about the height of a door. By standing near the recess and pressing on the floor a section of tiles 76cm long and 45cm wide pivots, and the opposite end lifts up. It is constructed of a stout block of oak, on top of which is an overlying surface of mortared brick, held within iron flanges. Though thick and heavy it is perfectly balanced and pivots within a wooden frame.

The hide below is entered by sitting on the floor (with legs down the hole) and sliding down a short slope – the old latrine chute – running under a dividing wall. Beyond the wall it is then possible to stand up in a 2.2m-high brick-vaulted chamber, complete with a wooden seat. The void as a whole is asymmetrical, with a variety of height and floor levels. Prior to conversion it was largely redundant, designed to lighten the load on the lower garderobe turret.[50] In addition, it may have been used for cleaning the chute.

This was the perfect place for a hide. It would have been difficult to detect, and the clever concealment and the seat suggest the hand of Nicholas Owen. Though unproven, it may once have communicated with the King's Room and a staircase by the entrance to a possible attic secret chapel in the north range (east of the gatehouse).

Squires recalled a conversation with an estate bailiff who remembered what he thought was a priest hole beneath the short flight of stairs leading to the King's Room. When open, it was apparently used as a wood store. In addition, he was told by Sir Henry Paston-Bedingfield that his father had remarked that he knew of another hiding place in the house, somewhere other than 'the dungeon'. Was this the aforementioned wood store, or some forgotten place, yet to be rediscovered? It is certainly possible. There were priest holes in the former hall range connecting the two wings (demolished c.1775) – and it is likely there were more.

Naturally, when a 1.2m-high brick-vaulted tunnel was uncovered in the early twentieth century, it was assumed to be a secret passageway for priests.

Located under the terrace on the north side of the mansion parallel to the moat, it was, of course, part of a complex system of drainage.

There is a final surprise in the atmospheric, nineteenth-century library. Visitors leave the room via a 'secret' gib door, embellished with dummy book spines.

Oxborough, near Swaffham PE33 9PS; National Trust, limited opening part year.

5. Ancient House (Sparrowe's House) Suffolk

The most famous building in Ipswich was originally a merchant's house. Its exterior is striking, particularly the elaborate mid-seventeenth-century pargeting (carvings) representing four continents. They were added by the prosperous Sparrowe family after they purchased the property in 1603. Ancient House remained in their hands for over two centuries and came also to be known as 'Sparrowe's House'.

At the east end of the front range there is a fifteenth-century hammer-beam roof. It belonged to the solar wing of a house whose hall was here (converted about 1670). A previously unknown roof space was uncovered 1801 when workmen cut into a wall to get to the roof tiles. Wooden angels and other religious items were found, and it is possible this was a long-forgotten secret chapel, created by adding a plastered floor. A window that is invisible from outside the building is evidence for this, but there is no longer any trace of a secret entrance.

A post-Restoration Charles II's coat of arms appears on the outside, and there is an unlikely tradition that the king hid in the attic following the Battle of Worcester.

30 Buttermarket, Ipswich IP1 1BH; shop with in-store museum.

LOST VAULTS
& FORGOTTEN CRYPTS

'One thing that often gets overlooked about old churches,' say the Churches Conservation Trust, 'is what's underneath them.'

The word 'vault' is an architectural term used to describe an arched ceiling construction, but it is commonly used to describe underground rooms and chambers, especially when vaulted. 'Lost vaults' are usually crypts – underground rooms (often burial chambers), generally below the east end of a church.

For example, a forgotten crypt was recently discovered at St Mary's Church in Redgrave, Suffolk. Set in open fields, this redundant Anglican church dates to the fourteenth century and is described as 'a gothic gem with tombs, statues and churchyard skulls' (referring to eighteenth-century gravestones with carved skulls peeping over the top).

Rumours about subterranean tombs and passages were confirmed when a stone slab in the chancel floor gave way, revealing steps and a brick-lined tunnel and a seventeenth-century crypt beneath the vestry. Inside were seventeen lead-lined coffins. The crypt was used for the lords of the manor, the Bacon family and, later, the Holts.

CENTRAL ENGLAND

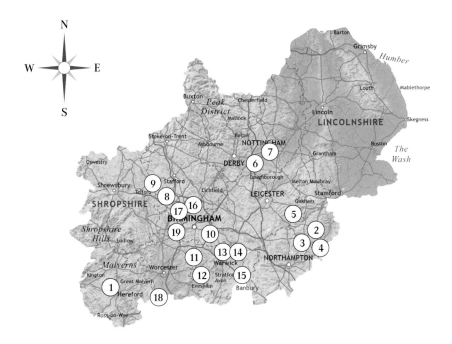

Central England's buildings contain an extraordinary record of the drama and romance of British history. Priest holes and secret tunnels recall the activities of Jesuits, plotters, kings and Cavaliers.

1. HAMPTON COURT HEREFORDSHIRE

Set amidst tranquil parkland on the River Lugg, this magnificent, castellated house has mid-fifteenth-century origins and predates its famous Surrey namesake. This Hampton Court is one of England's best kept secrets and was built by Sir Rowland Lenthall (d. 1450), a knight in Henry IV's court. In 1510 the manor house and land were sold to Justice of the King's Bench, Sir Humphrey Coningsby (d. 1535) and Hampton Court remained in the family until 1810.

The atmospheric house is full of interest, and the library boasts a difficult-to-spot nineteenth-century gib door with dummy book spines. In addition, a walk around the vast and beautiful gardens is highly recommended. Following years of neglect they were recently restored incorporating a pitch black 'secret tunnel' between the maze and the waterfall in the wonderful sunken garden. When you reach the waterfall there is another surprise: a rock-cut passage allowing visitors to walk behind it. Not ancient, but sure to delight!

Hope-Under-Dinmore, Leominster HR6 0PN; private house open to the public, open part year.

2. BOUGHTON HOUSE NORTHAMPTONSHIRE

Described as the 'English Versailles', Boughton House is undeniably magnificent. A former monastic building, it was purchased and converted into a house in 1528 by Sir Edward Montagu, Lord Chief Justice to King Henry VIII. Most of the present house is attributed to the ambitious and extravagant courtier the Hon. Ralph Montagu, 1st Duke of Montagu (1638–1709).

The house boasts a rare sliding panel, one of many fascinating antiquities. Beloved of nineteenth-century novelists, sliding panels are associated with mystery and intrigue. Given the Ralph Montagu's eccentric character and colourful career, its presence seems appropriate.

Montagu was a scheming courtier to Charles II, 'as arrant a knave as any in his time' wrote Jonathan Swift. Much of his rise is attributed to his skill as a seducer and manipulator of wealthy women – despite being described as 'of a middle stature, inclining to fat' with a 'coarse, dark complexion'. Montagu served as ambassador to France in the 1660s and had simultaneous affairs with both the king's former mistress, Barbara Palmer, 1st Duchess of Cleveland (1640–1709) and her teenage daughter Anne Lennard, Countess of Sussex (1661–1721). To add insult to injury, the king acknowledged that the young countess was one of his illegitimate daughters.

Having found out that Montagu was sleeping with her daughter, a furious Duchess of Cleveland wrote a letter to the king describing Montagu's lechery and scheming. Eager to defend himself, Montagu returned to England without leave and so was dismissed from his posts in 1678.

In an atmosphere of anti-Catholicism and political instability following the Popish Plot, Montagu's response was to secure a seat in the Commons to bring about the impeachment of the Earl of Danby by revealing to the Commons secret letters from Danby (as Lord Treasurer) to Paris. They were highly incriminating. Danby had reluctantly played a key role in the king's secret negotiations to pry money from Louis XIV of France in return for supporting French peace proposals (shortly after Parliament had voted to provide money for a war).

Fearful of arrest, Montagu fled to France but returned when James II ascended to the throne. He then switched his affiliation to William III (of Orange) and married the very rich (but insane) Elizabeth Cavendish (1654–1734). Montagu wooed her by posing as the Emperor of China!

Did Montagu commission the sliding panel? Located in an early eighteenth-century portion of the house, it is set into a thick wall next to a door, runs in grooves and has a pulley and counterbalancing weight. On giving an upward push to the beading, a section of panel the size of a door slides up into the wall to reveal a space 1.8m deep and a lofty 9m high. There may have been a way into or out of a cupboard in the floor above, but if this was the case, no evidence remains.

Kettering NN14 1BJ; private house open to the public, open part year. House open to groups (by appointment) all year round.

3. Lyveden New Bield Northamptonshire

A miraculous survival, Lyveden New Bield is an unfinished Elizabethan summer house replete with Catholic symbolism. The house was commissioned by the recusant Thomas Tresham of Rushton Hall (b. 1534), father of gunpowder plotter, Francis Tresham (c.1567–1605).

The unfinished house looks much as it did when workers downed tools in 1605, shortly after Thomas died with debts totalling £11,500 (a portion of which were recusancy related).

Nineteenth-century architect and architectural historian J.A. Gotch surveyed the house and noted that at the south entrance were the remains of a subterranean passage that had a strongly barred door. It led south-west and was probably a drain. However, such drains, as we have seen, are useful emergency exits and it is likely some were designed with this in mind.

Near Oundle PE8 5AT; National Trust, limited opening part year.

4. Drayton House Northamptonshire

Built around a fourteenth-century core attributed to Simon de Drayton, Drayton House was the seat of the Mordaunts, earls of Peterborough from 1628. It has a small hiding place not high enough to stand in, reached by a modern trapdoor in the floor of a room above the State Bedroom and lit by the lower portion of a tall window (not visible from the outside).

Referring to foreign Catholic seminary priests he believed frequented the house, the Protestant statesman Sir Robert Cecil described Drayton as 'a receptacle of most dangerous persons'. Indeed, Henry Mordaunt, 4th Baron Mordaunt of Turvey (c. 1564–1609) was given a fine of 10,000 marks (£6,666) and imprisoned for a year in the Tower of London on suspicion of being privy to the Gunpowder Plot.

Lowick, near Kettering NN14 3BB; private house, group visits by prior written appointment.

5. RUSHTON HALL NORTHAMPTONSHIRE

Robert Catesby formulated his plan to blow up Parliament at Ashby St Ledgers,[51] but there is another Northamptonshire house of significance in the history of the Gunpower Plot..

Magnificent Grade I listed Rushton Hall was where Charles Dickens conceived the idea for *Great Expectations* and was the seat of the Catholic Tresham family from 1438. Francis Tresham (1567–1605), son of recusant politician Sir Thomas Tresham (1543–1605), was another of the Gunpowder Plot conspirators.

During repairwork in 1828, a door lintel was moved and a book fell to the ground. It was part of an important collection of prohibited books and papers apparently hidden by Francis Tresham at the time of the Gunpowder Plot and now housed in the British Library. The small space in which they were concealed was 1.5m long and 38cm wide.

In the north-west corner of the park there is a delightful English Heritage-owned, three-storey folly called Triangular Lodge where plotters are rumoured to have met. It was designed by Sir Thomas and constructed between 1593 and 1597. Its form and measurements are directed by the number three (symbolising the Holy Trinity). On the entrance front is the inscription '*Tres Testimonium Dant*' ('there are three that give witness'), a biblical quotation from St John's Gospel referring to the Trinity and a pun on Sir Thomas' name. Here behind the fireplace on the top floor is a windowless, triangular space that was formerly inaccessible. Its purpose – if it had one – is unknown.

Rumour has it that a secret tunnel led from the hall to the folly, and when a drain was being put in the hall cellar, a stone slab with an iron ring was found. The space below had been filled with rubble.

Desborough Road, Rushton, Kettering NN14 1RR; now a hotel. Rushton Triangular Lodge in the former parkland is owned by English Heritage and open part year.

6. THRUMPTON HALL NOTTINGHAMSHIRE

Incorporating elements of an earlier manor house, the former seat of the Powdrill family combines historic charm with evolved Jacobean elegance.

Staunch Roman Catholics, the Powdrills lost Thrumpton after they were implicated in the Babington Plot of 1586 to assassinate the Protestant Queen Elizabeth and replace her with her Roman Catholic cousin, Mary (plot leader Anthony Babington was a family friend and lived at the nearby Kingston-on-Soar estate).

In 1927 former owner Rev. Frederick Ernest Charles Byron (a relative of Lord Byron) decided to investigate the tradition of a secret staircase from a ground-floor room. A section of eighteenth-century panelling was found to be removable and revealed an ancient, narrow staircase leading to the room above. Since the stairs were found to be older than the panelling, they must have been uncovered when it was installed and largely forgotten about, hence the tradition's survival.

The secret staircase occupies a projecting bay (the remainder of which is taken up by chimneys stacks) and was lit by two small windows. A trapdoor was constructed at its foot, with some rough quarried steps down into a small, brick-vaulted secret chamber off the cellar below. Incorporating a stone seat, it is 2m long, a little less than 1m wide and 1.2m high. The chamber was created in the thickness of a wall and concealed from the cellar by a plastered-over brick wall.

The ingenious nature of this well-hidden hide, the thoughtful stone seat and a tradition that Father Garnet was concealed here suggest the hand of the master priest-hole maker, Nicholas Owen.

Thrumpton NG11 0AX; private house, hosts various events, group tours by appointment.

7. Nottingham Castle Nottinghamshire

There is a veritable labyrinth of man-made caves, chambers and other features cut into sandstone here, parts of which are yet to be explored. Two caves under Castle Rock are perhaps the city's most famous.

Mortimer's Hole ran from the upper bailey of the old castle down to Brewhouse Yard and Ye Olde Trip to Jerusalem pub. It acquired its name after Edward III's men, led by the castle's constable, William Eland, used the then secret tunnel to sneak into the castle to capture the rebellious marcher lord, Roger de Mortimer (1287−1330). He was bound, gagged and taken to the Tower of London, dramatically ushering in Edward's personal reign.

After suffering defeat at the Battle of Neville's Cross in 1346, David II of Scotland (1324−71) was allegedly held here. According to tradition, he was imprisoned in a 9m by 4m, 4m-high rectangular chamber known as King David's Dungeon, part of a system of caves and passageways called Romylowe's Cave.

Nottingham NG1 6EL; museum, castle open seven days a week throughout the summer, limited opening November to February. Cave tours incur an additional fee.

'Boscobel' derives from *Bosco-bello*, Italian for 'in the midst of fair woods'. Both the house and the surrounding woodland played a major role in one of the most romantic stories in English history.[52]

L-shaped with two principal storeys, Boscobel began as a sixteenth-century, timber-framed farmhouse. In 1632 it was converted into a hunting lodge by John Giffard, the wealthy owner of several estates (including nearby White Ladies Priory). An original wattle and daub panel may be seen on the east wall of the hall.

The Giffards were staunch Roman Catholics and had access to a well-established network of safe houses. Boscobel was one of them, and it became a refuge for Catholic-aligned Royalists during the English Civil War. Indeed, following the disastrous Battle of Wigan Lane (25 August 1651) and a week prior to the defeat of Charles II's army at the Battle of Worcester (3 September 1651) the injured Earl of Derby (a Royalist) was taken in by Boscobel's Catholic caretakers, the Pendrells.

Following the Battle of Worcester, Charles fled in the company of the aforementioned earl, Lord Wilmot, Charles Giffard (the owner of the Boscobel Estate) and others. Derby suggested they go to Boscobel, but Giffard recommended White Ladies Priory, a short distance away (also under the custodianship of the Pendrells). Here the king was disguised as a farm labourer,

Boscobel House and the Royal Oak.

'in a coarse noggen shirt, with breeches of green coarse cloth and a doeskin leather doublet'.

With a £1,000 price on his head and with Parliamentarian soldiers in the area, Charles spent the next day hiding in nearby Spring Coppice wood with Richard Pendrell ('Trusty Dick'). He later recalled the hardships, 'In this wood I stayed all day without meat or drink and by great fortune it rained all the time which hindered them, as I believe, from coming into the wood to search for men that might be fled there.'

After dark, Charles and Pendrell travelled to Upper Madeley, Shropshire (since it had secret hiding places), hoping to cross the River Severn into Wales where support for the king was strong. However, on being told that the river crossings were closely guarded they were forced to return to Boscobel. They arrived at about 3 am on 6 September. William Careless (a Catholic Colonel who had fought at Worcester) had arrived the same day. It was he who suggested Charles should spend the day hiding in the bowl of a nearby pollarded oak tree (later named The Royal Oak), since Parliamentarian troops would be scouring the area and Boscobel's priest holes might not stand up to a daytime search.

Charles agreed, and the exhausted monarch slept much of the time, supported by Careless. That night the king spent a cramped night in one of Boscobel's priest holes before moving to Moseley Old Hall, north of Wolverhampton.

Boscobel's main hide has long been considered the one in which the king spent the night, as attested to by this wholly unscientific account from Mrs Sarah Brown's *Boscobel and its Visitors: Recollections by the Custodian* (1910):

> We had a lady and gentleman staying at Boscobel with their three daughters. They had often supposed there were ghosts here, and wondered if they would ever see them ... In the night I was awakened by screams, and got up and went to see what was the matter. I found them all up, and the young-est in hysterics, declaring that she had seen a man slowly emerging from the King's hiding-place ... We had to search the house thoroughly and her mother had to stay with her for the rest of the night.

There is, however, better evidence that the aforementioned hide was the king's. It is located off the top attic or Cheese Room (so called because cheese was stored here) – the former secret chapel. There is a small square trapdoor at the top of the stair here. Now obvious, it is said that straw was spread on the floor to conceal it. Another tradition maintains that cheeses were stacked on top of it, and that the pungent smell rendered bloodhounds useless.

The chamber itself is 1.5m deep and not much more than 1m square – extremely uncomfortable for a monarch who stood 6ft 2in (1.87m) tall. However, the hide is well constructed and would have been difficult to discover. It was made by building a wall across a small store room in the floor below and is lined with hair plaster to deaden sound.

One of the best contemporary sources of information on the events at Boscobel is Father Thomas Blount's *Boscobel* (1651), in which he says the king could survey the road from Tong to Brewood from his hide and that he had a 'gallery to walk in'. The only window matching this description adjoins the hide. What is more, historian Michael Hodgetts suggests that since the attic runs the full length of the wing it 'could fairly be called a gallery'. He goes further, pointing out that this was the hide shown to the antiquarian William Stukely in 1713, when members of the Pendrell family were still living at Boscobel. Furthermore, *A True Narrative and Relation* (which draws on the Pendrell's recollections) described the king's hide as a place between two walls (which it is), 'contrived at the building of the house'. This leaves little room for doubt.

There is a fireside closet in the Squire's Bedroom on the first floor, built into a large chimney stack on the west side of the house. Lit by a small window, it is accessed via a door that was supposedly secret. According to a tradition, the right-hand side of the closet gave entry into a mysterious shaft that ran from the top floor to the basement. The story sounds far-fetched – but there *is* a secret here. Amidst the boards a trapdoor between the joists covers a space roughly 1m square – perhaps a small priest hole. Below this, but not connected with it, is a room that can only be entered through a small door at the top of some steps in the garden. Of, course there is an unfounded tradition that the two spaces were joined to create a bolt hole.

See also A Great Escape ... (p. 173).

Bishops Wood ST19 9AR; English Heritage, open part year.

9. LILLESHALL ABBEY SHROPSHIRE

The high walls and graceful arches of the twelfth-century Augustinian abbey of Lilleshall stand in deeply rural surroundings. Around the time of the Dissolution the abbey and its estate were acquired by the wool merchant, James Leveson (d. 1549). The abbey was then converted into a secular residence and became the Leveson family's seat. During the Civil War, Sir Richard Leveson (1598–1661) supported the Royalist cause, and the abbey was garrisoned for the king. Then, in August 1645, it was bombarded and stormed by Parliamentarian forces, causing great damage.

For a time, the abbey remains were at the centre of a mystery. It all began in 1928 when a custodian's family moved into the abbey cottage and were disturbed by nocturnal 'rumblings and moanings', along with muffled footsteps.

At first they were attributed to miners from Lilleshall Colliery, but the mystery deepened after the custodian's son saw the 'shadow of a person' and the family were informed there were no active works under the abbey.

Some thought the sounds were connected to the tradition of a Civil War-era secret passageway to Longford Hall, an unfeasibly distant 3.2km away. The Rev. W.M.L Evans, then the Rector of Saxby, wrote that he distinctly remembered an 'old passage' from a time when he was a tutor at the adjacent Lilleshall Hall, some thirty years previously. It seemed there was substance to the rumours.

In 1932 the owners offered a reward of £50 to any dowser or archaeologist who could solve the mystery. The plot thickened when exploratory excavations beneath the abbey's east window revealed human remains, possibly from the Civil War, including skulls. Then, a local newspaper wrote that a dowser had received a 'violent shock' that led to the discovery of an underground passage. Sadly, no further details were given. Writing around the same time, Squires was dismissive, 'Fifty pounds seems a large sum of money to pay to locate what cannot be more than a sewer or water conduit.'

So what caused the mysterious sounds? It turns out that the stories about subterranean passages were correct – to an extent.

Certainly, old drains are associated with the abbey and a 65m, late eighteenth-century canal tunnel at nearby Hugh's Bridge might have contributed to secret passageway rumours. More significant, however, are some very old mine workings hereabouts. In fact, subsidence has severely damaged some of the remains, and during the 1960s the walls of the church had to be shored up to protect them. That subsidence can induce a variety of sounds (including rumbling) is a well-attested fact.

Newport TF10 9HW; English Heritage, open all year.

10. BADDESLEY CLINTON HALL WARWICKSHIRE

With its two-arched, eighteenth-century bridge and showpiece crenellated gatehouse, Baddesley Clinton epitomises the romantic notion of a medieval manor house. The present fifteenth-century house is built of stone and is set around three sides of a courtyard (a fourth range to the north was pulled down in the early eighteenth century to open up the courtyard view). A spring-fed moat, dug by the Clintons who settled here in the thirteenth century, completes the idyllic scene.

In 1438, Baddesley Clinton was sold to wealthy Warwickshire lawyer (and later, Under Treasurer of England) John Brome (c. 1410–68). It was either John or his son, Nicholas, who built the present house.

John Brome was a supporter of the Lancastrian king, Henry VI. After the accession of the Yorkist claimant, Edward IV, he lost his court appointments and was murdered at White Friars, London by John Herthill (the Earl of Warwick's Steward). Hell-bent on revenge, Nicholas Brome eventually murdered his father's assailant.

Legend has it that Nicholas Brome was prone to violent rages. Henry Ferrers, a later owner of the house, told how Brome came home unexpectedly and 'slew ye minister of Baddesley Church findinge him in his parlour chockinge his wife under ye chinne'. Brome was pardoned for the killing and, as penance, commissioned new steeples at Baddesley Clinton and Packwood churches.[53]

When Nicholas died in 1517 his second daughter married Sir Edward Ferrers (d. 1536), initiating more than four centuries of Ferrers ownership. The Elizabethan antiquary and MP Henry Ferrers owned the house from 1564 to 1633 and did much to embellish it. Although Henry was a devout Roman Catholic, he was never penalised for his religion and largely kept out of trouble. That said, he must have known about the activities of his tenants.

Between 1588 and 1592 Henry let Baddesley Clinton to Eleanor Brooksby (c. 1560–1625) and her unmarried sibling, Anne Vaux (c. 1562–c. 1637). For years the wealthy pair rented properties to establish safe houses for priests and, in mid-October 1591, Baddesley Clinton was almost certainly the venue for the Jesuits' twice yearly secret conference.

However, a few days before it began, a drunken pursuivant named Hodgkins demanded admission and was kept waiting while incriminating items were hidden. Incensed (and no doubt suspicious), he threatened to return with a posse within ten days. A raid, it seemed, was imminent.

A view of the north-east corner of Baddesley Clinton showing the Gatehouse Bridge.
Copyright National Trust Images/Andrew Butler

The events that followed were recorded by Father John Gerard in his *Autobiography* and in a letter by Jesuit superior Henry Garnet to his superior in Rome, Claudio Acquaviva – though neither reveal the name of the house. Gerard wrote of a house in Warwickshire 'almost a hundred miles from London', kept by the priest-harbouring sisters. Its main secret hiding place was unusual, described as a 'very cleverly built sort of cave'. Baddesley Clinton is some 159km (99 miles) from London, very secluded and has a hiding place that fits the bill perfectly.

Unable to get word to the Jesuits who were on their way, Garnet decided to continue as planned. Nine were present as the conference got under way. At the final dinner Jesuit Superior Father Henry Garnet urged those present to disperse quickly once their business was concluded, adding 'I do not guarantee your safety any longer.'

After dinner, four priests mounted their horses and rode off into the night, leaving five of the leading Jesuits, two secular priests and two or three laymen. Gerard described the events of the early hours of the next morning:

> About five o'clock, when Father Southwell was beginning Mass, and the others and myself were at meditation, I heard a bustle at the house door. Directly after, I heard cries and oaths poured forth against the servant for refusing admittance. The fact was that four priest-hunters, or pursuivants as they are called, with drawn swords, were trying to break down the door and force an entrance. The faithful servant withstood them, otherwise we should have been all made prisoners. But by this time Father Southwell had heard the uproar, and, guessing what it meant, had at once taken off his vestments and stripped the altar; while we strove to seek out everything belonging to us, so that there might be nothing found to betray the lurking of a priest. We did not even wish to leave boots and swords lying about, which would serve to show there had been many guests, though none of them appeared. Hence many of us were anxious about our beds, which were still warm, and only covered according to custom previous to being made. Some therefore went and turned their beds over, so that the colder part might deceive anybody who put his hand in to feel. Thus while the enemy was shouting and bawling outside, and our servants were keeping the door, saying that the mistress of the house, a widow, had not yet got up, but that she was coming directly and would give them an answer, we profited by the delay to stow away ourselves and all our baggage in a cleverly contrived hiding place.

Gerard explained that the secret hiding place was, 'underground, covered with water at the bottom, so that I was standing with my feet in water all the time'.

Finally, the priest hunters were let in. The raid was more akin to burglary than a professional, systematic search. For four hours they turned the house upside down, looking everywhere and prying into all the dark corners with candles. But it was not a success. Anne Vaux paid them off, and they left.

> When they were gone, and were now some way off, so that there was no fear of their returning, as they sometimes do, a lady came and summoned out of the den not one but many Daniels.

Five or more men had hidden in the main sewer. It was entered via an old garderobe chute in the sacristy next to the chapel, where now there is a modern trapdoor. The passage runs east–west under the entire length of the west range with an additional section where it turns east under the old brewhouse (it probably continued under the now demolished north range). For most of its 26m the passage is just over 1m high and not much more than 0.5m wide.

There can be no doubt that the sewer was converted to secrecy – and probably by Nicholas Owen. At the south-west end a great stone slab the width and height of the passage was slotted into grooves near the drain exit to create a sluice gate. It was probably raised and lowered from the turret room above, allowing the sewer to be periodically cleaned. The passage could be sealed and opened at will and in conjunction with changes to the level of the moat – a most useful security feature. Even more significant are the unmistakable remains of thick walls that were not part of the original passage. They suggest that a section of the sewer below the sacristy was isolated from the rest, and that it was only accessible from the garderobe chute. Water seepage would have made the passage damp to say the least (thus fitting Gerard's description). The loopholes, meanwhile, were blocked and all but invisible from the outside. The few that remain blocked today illustrate the efficacy of the camouflage.

In addition to the original sacristy entrance, today there are two further entrances from the ground floor. One is in the kitchen, covered by a glass viewing panel. The other is a trapdoor in the old brewhouse, where there is a flight of Victorian steps.

Guidebooks mention two further priest holes. One can be found in the roof above a closet off a bedroom in the gatehouse block. It is a roughly 2m by 1m, 1m high lath and plaster hutch with two wooden benches. The hide is lined with hair plaster and is missing its camouflaged door from the roof space. A final (possible) priest hole is a small room beneath the reputedly haunted Library Room (where Nicholas Brome is said to have murdered the priest). Apparently, it was accessed through a fireplace in the Great Parlour, but can now be viewed through a door in the panelling above the 'moat room' fireplace at the north end of the east range.

In October 1591, following a secret conference of Jesuits, five or more men hid in this converted sewer. It was entered via an old garderobe chute in the sacristy next to the chapel, where now there is a modern trapdoor. The priest hole, formerly a medieval sewer, beneath the kitchen, Baddesley Clinton, Warwickshire. *Copyright National Trust Images/ James Dobson*

Plan of Baddesley Clinton Hall showing the location of its sewer.

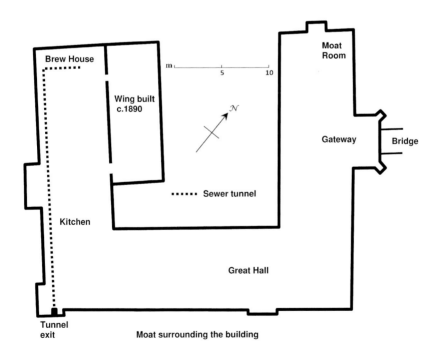

Brew House

Wing built c.1890

Moat Room

Gateway

Bridge

Kitchen

Sewer tunnel

Great Hall

Tunnel exit

Moat surrounding the building

An unlikely tradition maintains that Guy Fawkes lived at Baddesley Clinton, partly because 'Vaux' and 'Fawkes' are pronounced in the same way (except for the initial letter). Add to this the fact that Henry Ferrers unwittingly let his Westminster house to a gunpowder plotter in 1604 – and one can see how the story arose.

Henry's poor judgement extended to matters of finance. He accrued large debts, and Baddesley Clinton changed little after his death. That, of course, is our gain.

Baddesley Clinton B93 0DQ; National Trust, open all year.

11. COUGHTON COURT WARWICKSHIRE

Set on the edge of the old Forest of Arden, this grand old house with its crenelated façade and imposing, fifteenth-century gatehouse has been the home of the Catholic Throckmorton family for more than six centuries. The family's history is remarkable. A former ambassador to France, Sir Nicholas Throckmorton (*c.* 1515–71) was a high-stakes schemer and was imprisoned for supporting Mary, Queen of Scots. His nephew, Sir Francis Throckmorton (1554–84) went further, and was a key conspirator in the Throckmorton Plot of 1583 to murder Queen Elizabeth I and install her half-sister Mary in her stead (as a consequence, he was executed). Coughton Court became a centre for Catholics in the time of Sir Robert Throckmorton (*c.* 1512–82) and his son and heir, Sir Thomas (1533–1614), and was frequented by Jesuit priests Henry Garnet and Edward Oldcorne (1561–1606).

Sir Thomas lent Coughton Court to the chief Gunpowder Plot conspirators, though he was absent on the cold early hours of 6 November 1605, when a group of them waited anxiously in the gatehouse Tower Room to hear news of the plot. It was here that arms, horses and ammunition had been stored, ready for the uprising that was meant to follow the destruction of king and Parliament.

In common with most Roman Catholic families, the Throckmortons were Royalists. However, Parliamentary forces took over the house in 1643 and it was heavily damaged during a Royalist bombardment. A further setback occurred when a rampaging mob of Protestants destroyed the east side of the courtyard during the Glorious Revolution of 1688.

Three sides of a sixteenth-century courtyard remain today along with three known priest holes. At least one is a *double* hide.

In the north-east corner of the Tower Room (the former secret chapel) beneath a closet in one of the hexagonal turrets is a 1m-square priest hole, under which is another secret compartment of a similar size to the upper one. When the lower hide was discovered in 1858, it was found to contain a rope ladder, three altar stones, straw bedding and some faded fragments of blue and yellow tapestry (now on display in the Tower Room). Of course, tradition embellishes fact and there is a story about a secret passageway from here to a house in the village. It probably stems from a blocked spiral staircase that was accessible via a moveable oak board in the lower hide's floor.

A second priest hole can be found next to the Dining Room and the Tribune (which leads from the Dining Room). Now entered through a moveable panel at the Tribune end, it is 2.3m long (including four steps, since the floor is above the level of the rooms outside), 1m wide, 2.2m high and lined with panelling (not original). Repairs in 1956 revealed a space beneath which showed signs of use, indicating that it might also have been a double hide.

Hodgetts casts doubt on the authenticity of a possible hide off an ante-room on the ground floor (below the Tribune). The panels in the room were brought from Harvington and fitted here in 1929. One of them was made to slide to provide a view of a small space labelled 'Bins' on eighteenth-century plans.

Numerous relics are kept in the house including a seventeenth-century cabinet with a secret recess for Mass equipment, family documents detailing recusancy-related issues, the shift in which Mary, Queen of Scots is said to have been beheaded, locks of hair from the Young and Old Pretenders and a chair reputedly made from the wood of the bed in which Richard III spent his last night before the Battle of Bosworth Field.

The Throckmorton family still resides here, but the house has been in the hands of the National Trust since 1945.

Alcester B49 5JA; National Trust, limited opening part year.

12. SALFORD HALL WARWICKSHIRE

◇◇◇

Guests at this Elizabethan-style country house are greeted by a huge Tudor fireplace, oak-panelled rooms and quaint, atmospheric passages.

Salford Hall is mostly built of stone around three sides of a narrow, open courtyard. It is thought the west range was built in the fifteenth century for the abbots of Evesham, though it was remodelled in the sixteenth century. The range contains the hall, which is entered through a projecting porch with a black and white timber-framed gable. The north and east ranges were built in local blue lias (limestone) by John Alderford (d. 1606), whose motto '*Moderata Durant*' ('Moderate things endure') appears above the north porch and is dated 1662 (a restorer's mistake – it originally said 1602).

The family had Roman Catholic leanings. Hodgetts notes that Alderford's second wife, Elizabeth Morgan, and her son-in-law and successor Charles Stanford, were returned as recusants in 1610. During the Civil War Charles' son and successor, John, was a Cavalier. He was killed in 1649.

During the early eighteenth century the Stanfords converted the ground floor of the north range into a chapel (served by Benedictine monks from 1727 until the end of that century). Then, during the first half of the nineteenth century, Salford Hall was occupied by a group of French Benedictine nuns, fugitives from the French Revolution. Afterwards, the hall was known as 'The Nunnery'.

Set around that time, *The Tragic Legend of Salford Hall* is a tale of uncertain origin about two English sisters, Wyom and Evra Hendon. After living in America for two years, they are taken to the hall by their father's business partner and apparent guardian, the mysterious Herbert Dingwall. He claims to know and admire the French abbess, Dame Burgoyne, and abruptly leaves the two children, who are around 11 and 13 years old, along with money for their care and mysterious instructions to place an advert in *The Times* when the eldest, Wyom, came of age.

The sisters are unusually close, and Evra is haunted by recurring dreams that they are to be parted. Sadly, this comes to pass.

At the appointed time the advert is placed in *The Times*. Then, a letter arrives for the abbess, instructing her to immediately send Wyom to 'Holt House, Graybourne, Buckinghamshire'. After much deliberation, the child is sent on her way. However, after hearing no word from the girl, the abbess learns that Holt House does not exist.

A distraught Evra begins to disappear from her bed at night. No one can locate her when this happens, despite all the doors being locked. The nuns search 'downstairs, everywhere; chapel, porch, passages, sleeping rooms, day rooms and cellars. But no Trace of Evra.'

They are utterly baffled. Evra explains:

I've been a long way from here a good many nights lately. I thought I heard Wyom calling me, so I got up and came down the stairs, and went along the passage that leads to the laundry; but it wasn't, for it had no window on the right, and it had no door at the end; it had a window at the end, but oh! It was such a long way off. At first I walk along the passage, then I ran, for I knew that Wyom was there, and that they were hurting her.

It transpires that Wyom is an heiress – and Dingwall a rogue. There is a supernatural twist, best understood by reading the book. Suffice to say, it was found that:

... with the aid of a good compass and a good map ... if the walls of the passage parallel to the chapel, on whichever side of the chapel the passage lay, could be extended for enough in a straight line, they would pass through the very house in which Wyom had been so nearly murdered.

Interestingly, there is no mention of Salford Hall's secret chamber. It can be found in a hallway on the top floor where there is a plain-looking, shallow cupboard in the thickness of the wall. It is lined with oak and has oak shelves, and any searcher would hardly give it a second glance. However, when pushed, the whole of the back, along with the shelves, swings backwards on concealed hinges to reveal a draughty, 1.5m-long chamber in the angle between the wall and the roof tiles. A hidden fastening secured the hide on the outside, and it could be bolted from within.

Evesham WR11 8UT; country house hotel, tours and events by arrangement.

13. St John's House Museum (formerly St John's Hospital) Warwickshire

◇◇

This lovely, two-storey Jacobean mansion is today run as a museum showcasing social history. Considered to be one of the most important historic buildings in Warwick, it was built on the site of the hospital of St John the Baptist, perhaps incorporating some of the structure. The hospital was founded during the reign of Henry II (1154–89) for the 'entertainment and reception of travellers, as well as those that were poor and infirm'.

Around the time of the Dissolution, whatever remained of the property passed to a veteran of the Tudor courts, Anthony Stoughton. In 1626 the house was remodelled by his grandson of the same name, Sir Anthony Stoughton (c. 1587–1656), and was held by the family until 1763. In 1788 St John's House passed to the Greville family when it was sold to George Greville, 2nd Earl of Warwick (1746–1816).

The interior boasts an original newel close-string staircase, late seventeenth-century panelling and some remaining timberwork in the rear elevation. In addition, there were two secret hiding places here. According to Squires, they were blocked up, but Allan Fea maintained there was a secret chamber behind one of the large panels in the hall, and that the other was in a little dressing-room off a former bedroom. The room was secret, and could only be reached through a sliding panel over the fireplace.

Warwick CV34 4NF; museum, limited opening all year.

14. WARWICK CASTLE WARWICKSHIRE

After a thousand years of turbulent history, this mighty medieval fortress has become one of Britain's most visited attractions. Formerly the ancestral home of the earls of Warwick, the castle sits on a small escarpment above the River Avon and looms large above the town. It began with an eleventh-century Norman keep, raised on the site of earlier, Saxon fortifications. However, most of the present exterior is mid-fourteenth century, when the castle was held by the Beauchamp family. Although Warwick 'the Kingmaker', Richard Neville, later succeeded to the estates and title, he made little impression.

Most of the interior dates from a period after James I granted the castle to the dramatist, poet and wealthy local Member of Parliament, Sir Fulke Greville (1554–1628). The castle had become dilapidated, and he spent £20,000 restoring it. Whilst on a trip to London in 1628, he was stabbed and killed by his own servant, Ralph Haywood (he had found out he did not feature in his master's will).

Squires mentioned a cutting in his possession about 'a door cunningly contrived in the rich panelling of the Green Drawing-room that leads to a secret staircase with a former exit on the river bank'.

The room in question is the most beautiful of the state rooms. Largely created in the seventeenth century, its green walls are adorned with many paintings, all set below a wonderful eighteenth-century coffered ceiling. Visitors should look out for a cleverly hidden door in one corner, concealed so it did not spoil the decorative panelling. Legend has it that William Greville, 7th Baron Brooke (1695–1727), brought here a maid servant whom he had made pregnant and pushed her down the spiral stair behind the door. According to the story, he went on to drown her in the River Avon.

The base of Caesar's Tower contains a dungeon with an oubliette and long-sealed rooms have recently been opened to the public: the Barbican Battlements with its deadly murder holes, the Captain's Room, the Bear Tower (complete with bear pit for bear baiting), the Watergate Tower (purportedly haunted by Sir Fulke Greville) and the Guard's Room in Guy's Tower. In addition, there is a secret passageway of sorts (a sally port). Well hidden, its door can be found around the side of the Clarence Tower.

Warwick CV34 4QU; Merlin Entertainments Group, open all year.

15. BILLESLEY MANOR WARWICKSHIRE

According to local tradition, Shakespeare wrote *As You Like It* here and had the run of the library as a boy. Some believe he married the pregnant Anne Hathaway at All Saints (the local church), and there is an unproven theory that he was related to the former lords of the manor via his maternal grandmother.

Located 6.4km west of Stratford-upon-Avon, the Trussell family held Billesley for 400 years (until 1588, when a hard-up Thomas Trussell turned to highway robbery and the estate was seized). Only faint traces remain of their earlier, moated house. However, the extant seventeenth-century, L-shaped manor house, now a hotel, has an interesting secret hiding place.

Fittingly, it is located in the beautifully panelled former library on the first floor (now Room 4 – the 'Shakespeare Room'). Here, in the west reveal of the doorway between the corner of the room and a panelled fireplace is a cupboard in the panelling. Inside the cupboard, there is a trapdoor in a false ceiling. This leads to a space over the doorway and on into a small secret chamber behind the fireplace panelling.

Billesley Manor.

Lined with hair plaster, the secret chamber is just over 1m wide and 1.5m high. There is said to be a peep hole from it via a slot in a central oval jewel ornament in the moulded fireplace overmantel. Tradition also speaks of a way from the hide up into the garrets.

Billesley B49 6NF; country house hotel.

16. ASTON HALL BIRMINGHAM

◇◇

Built between 1618 and 1635 for Sir Thomas Holte (1571–1654), this imposing Jacobean house is located next to Aston Villa Football Club. A Royalist, Sir Thomas famously entertained Charles I here for one night in October 1642, some seven years after the hall was completed.

The house was attacked by Parliamentarian troops from Coventry in 1643 and the damage is still evident. In several places are the marks of cannon balls, one of which penetrated the brick walls and damaged the magnificent Jacobean oak staircase, still shown in its splintered state. On the ground floor, beneath the third section of the staircase, there is a curiosity. A large, beautifully carved wooden porter's chair stands against the wall – a chair with a secret. It swings around on hinges to reveal a 1.8m by 3m space.

This 'secret' chamber is a nineteenth-century folly, and for a time a female human skeleton of unknown provenance was kept there. Squires recalled an octogenarian custodian who delighted in opening up the mysterious door, detaching the skull and placing it in unsuspecting visitor's hands. On one of those occasions, a nervous young lady fainted, and the subsequent letters of complaint led to the skeleton's removal.

Birmingham B6 6JD; museum, open part year Tuesday to Sunday.

17. MOSELEY OLD HALL WEST MIDLANDS

◇◇

Do not be fooled by the plain exterior. This late Elizabethan house *oozes* historical significance.

Henry Pitt built Moseley Old Hall shortly after he purchased the estate in 1583. After his death in 1602, it passed to his daughter, Alice (d. 1668). It was her second marriage to Thomas Whitgreave (1568–1626) that established the Roman Catholic Whitgreave family at Moseley. Alice's son, another Thomas, played a major role in British history. He saved a king.

On Sunday, 7 September 1651, a fugitive Charles II had once again found himself at Boscobel House. His journey was not going to plan and he had aborted an attempt to cross the Severn into Wales. Now, at last, there was good news. John Pendrell had found Lord Wilmott at the house of the afore-mentioned Mr Whitgreave. What is more, Moseley Old Hall had 'a very secure hiding place'. The king, it was agreed, could be moved there.

Late in the evening of Sunday, 7 September 1651 Charles set off, initially in the company of all five Pendrell brothers from Boscobel and Charles Giffard's servant (and brother-in-law to the Pendrells), Francis Yates. The men were armed with bills, pikestaves and pistols. On reaching Penford Mill, and having completed the most dangerous part of the journey along minor roads, William, Humphrey and George Pendrell departed with the horse. When Charles realised he had not thanked them, he called the brothers back and gave them his hand to kiss. 'My troubles,' he said, 'make me forget myself; I thank you all.' The final few kilometres of dark countryside were traversed using footpaths, which were safer.

Whitgreave's priest, Father John Huddleston, waited anxiously in an adjoin-ing field. At the request of Lord Wilmot, Whitgreave waited near the door of the orchard, behind Moseley Old Hall.

The party arrived a little before midnight. When Charles came through the orchard door with the remaining Pendrells, Mr Whitgreave saw 'he was so habitted like one of them, that I could not tell which was hee'. Without paus-ing, Charles headed straight for the heavily studded back door to a small spiral stair (where Lord Wilmot was holding a lamp). From there, he was escorted to Mr Huddleston's room – now known as the King's Room. Mr Whitgreave escorted the Pendrells into the buttery to eat and drink, 'that I might dispatch them away, and secure the house'.

Huddleston then came to fetch Mr Whitgreave to the chamber, where Charles and Lord Wilmot were waiting. Almost immediately, Charles asked to inspect the hide, which had been prepared before his arrival. From his bedroom, a door near the fireplace led into a tall closet, within which, next to some flues, there was a trapdoor made from two short pieces of floorboard and securable from the underside. The trap led to a partly hair plaster-lined chamber about 1.5m by 1.5m and a little over 1m deep, with a ledge at one end forming a step. Praising its quality, Charles returned to the bedroom, where Whitgreave and Huddleston washed his blistered feet. Having taken some wine and biscuits, his sprits lifted and the three men chatted for an hour before Charles retired.

The next day all the servants except the Catholic cook, Elizabeth Smith, were sent on errands and were told that Huddleston was not well and that no one was to enter his room except Whitgreave and his elderly mother, Alice. Feigning personal apprehension as a Roman Catholic priest, Huddleston instructed his three pupils to watch the road from the attics. Meanwhile, Charles benefitted from these arrangements and was able to rest on Huddleston's bed and plan the next stage of his journey.

By the next day (Tuesday, 9 September), Charles had regained some strength. A little closet over the porch of the door that enters the hall was used as a study. Charles talked here with Huddleston, and from the window watched two fleeing soldiers pass the gate on the road from Wolverhampton, one of whom he recognised to be a Highlander of his own regiment. Since the closet over the hall porch still exists, its description puts the location of Mr Huddleston's room – and the king's hiding place – beyond doubt.

Towards evening, Charles had a narrow escape. Elizabeth Smith came running to the stairs and cried, 'Soldiers, soldiers are coming!' Charles jumped out of bed and went to the hide. Whitgreave assisted him and made sure he was secure. Then, he went out into the street to talk to the soldiers. They were aggressive and accused him of fighting for the Royalists at Worcester:

> ... after much dispute with them, and by the neighbours being informed of their false information, that I was not there, being very ill a great while, they let mee goe; but till I saw them clearly all gone forth of the town, I returned not; but as soon as they were, I returned to release him.

Later, Whitgreave learned that while he was arguing with the soldiers, Southall the 'Priest Catcher' had approached a smith who was busy shoeing horses in the yard. He had offered him £1,000 to reveal the king's whereabouts.

That night, wrote Whitgreave, Charles asked Father Huddleston to show him the secret chapel, for 'he knew he was a priest, and he need not fear him, for if it pleased God to restore him to his kingdom, we should never need more privacies'. It seems the pair had formed a bond. In 1685, Huddlestone is said to have administered the sacrament to Charles on his deathbed, according to the rites of the Roman Catholic Church.

The aforementioned chapel is located in the attic above the King's Room. Nearby, high in the gable above the King's Room closet and the hall porch, there is a small secret hiding place or 'conveyance' for concealing items used at Mass.

The closet off the King's Room is today a passage to another room. On the King's Room side its wooden door has been camouflaged in dereference to a tradition that it was secret, supposedly indistinguishable from the panels that once covered the entire wall. Stepping inside, visitors may view the historic priest hole. It has survived largely intact and even retains its original trapdoor.

In 1870, the exterior of Moseley Old Hall was entirely refaced in brick, hiding the original black and white timber exterior. The interior, however, retains much of its authenticity with original panelling, timber framing, oak flooring and seventeenth-century oak furniture (including the actual bed on which Charles II slept). In addition, there are contemporary portraits of the king, along with those who shared his adventures.

See also A Great Escape (p. 173).

Wolverhampton WV10 7HY; National Trust, open part year.

18. BISMORTON COURT WORCESTERSHIRE

For three centuries this partly half-timbered, moated manor house was the seat of the distinguished Nanfan family. Bismorton was much altered by Giles Nanfan (d. 1614) and most of the internal architectural features (apart from recent alterations) are attributed to him. In the later fifteenth century, Giles, a known recusant, married Elizabeth, the Jesuit priest Robert Southwell's sister. Were there priest holes here? Almost certainly.

One candidate holds up to eight people (standing) and now appears as a closet by the side of a fireplace in the panelled and atmospheric Council Chamber. According to tradition, it was connected to a secret passageway that ran under the moat. Even more unlikely is a story that the Lollard leader Sir John Oldcastle (d. 1417) and Queen Margaret of Anjou (1430–82) hid here.

Malvern WR13 6JS; private house, bespoke tours by appointment.

19. HARVINGTON HALL WORCESTERSHIRE

An Elizabethan pile with red-brick chimneys and lofty gables rises out of a tranquil, reedy moat. 'Surely Hood's Haunted House or Poe's House of Usher stands before us, and we cannot get away from the impression that a mystery is wrapped within its walls,' wrote Allan Fea as he surveyed Harvington Hall at the beginning of the last century. It remains the typical moated grange of fiction: rustic, melancholy and, inevitably, haunted. But there is more – for within these walls are the best-preserved and most complete set of priest holes in Britain.

The moat and artificial island have thirteenth-century origins while the present, irregular, L-plan house conceals a timber-framed, H-plan building built in about the fourteenth century. Parts of this early manor house remain standing in the centre block, under later brickwork.

Harvington was owned by a series of Roman Catholics who, of course, kept priests here. In 1529, it was sold to a wealthy lawyer named Sir John Pakington and either his nephew, also named John (1523–78), or more probably the latter's son, Humphrey (1555–1631), remodelled the house between 1580 and 1600, enlarging it around a central courtyard and refacing the walls in brick. Around this time, Harvington was equipped with priest holes, some of which may reasonably be attributed to Nicholas Owen.

Following Humphrey's death the house passed to his daughter, Lady Mary Yate (d. 1696), then in the year of her death to her granddaughter, another Mary Yate. She married Sir Robert Throckmorton of Coughton Court, Warwickshire (p. 96).

HOW TO FIND PRIEST HOLES

In 1606 Robert Cecil, 1st Earl of Salisbury and James I's chief minister and spymaster gave succinct instructions for searching Hindlip Hall, Worcestershire:

> In the search, observe the parlour where they use to dine and sup; in the east part of that parlour it is conceived there is some vault, which to discover you must take care to draw down the wainscot, whereby the entry into the vault may be discovered. The lower parts of the house must be tried with a broach, by putting the same into the ground some foot or two, to try whether there may be perceived some timber, which, if there be, there must be some vault underneath it. For the upper rooms, you must observe whether they be more in breadth than the lower rooms, and look in which places the rooms be enlarged; by pulling up some boards, you may discover some vaults. Also, if it appear that there be some corners to the chimneys, and the same boarded, if the boards be taken away there will appear some. If the walls seem to be thick, and covered with wainscot, being tried with a gimlet, if it strike not the wall, but go through, some suspicion is to be had thereof. If there be any double loft, some two or three feet, one above another, in such places any may be harboured privately. Also, if there be a loft towards the roof of the house, in which there appears no entrance out of any other place or lodging, it must of necessity be opened and looked into, for these be ordinary places of hovering [hiding].[54]

A search could be followed by a watch:

> Fifty or sixty men, and sometimes more, and these with guns and bills ... and this they keep for many days. Because they can find nothing, and seem to make a noise as though they did depart; then will they go softly into the chambers ... and knock softly at every wall, willing the good man to come forth, for now the searchers are gone, thanks be to God.[55]

Harvington Hall.

The Throckmortons had little use for the house and, in about 1700, demolished the north and west ranges. By the end of the nineteenth century it had fallen into severe disrepair.

Fortunately, in November 1923, a Mrs Ellen Ryan Ferris of King's Norton, Birmingham bought the old hall and donated it to the Roman Catholic Archdiocese of Birmingham. Subsequently, it was restored.

What a loss it would have been! A maze of doors, passages and staircases lead off at all angles and would have puzzled the most experienced pursuivant. 'No two floors levels seem to be alike,' wrote Squires, 'and it is so full of queer corners that even to plot the place roughly on paper would seem an endless task.'

Withdrawing Room

Cross the bridge and enter the main gateway and you will see a small hole in a diagonal timber. It indirectly communicates with a priest hole in the Withdrawing Room and Squires proposed it was used for passing food or for communication, and that it could have been concealed. However, this seems unlikely since the gateway would have been well guarded during a raid. It is possible there was a hitching ring for tethering horses, or the hole could be related to former drawbridge fittings.

Nine Worthies Passage, Harvington Hall.

Section of west wing, Harvington Hall.

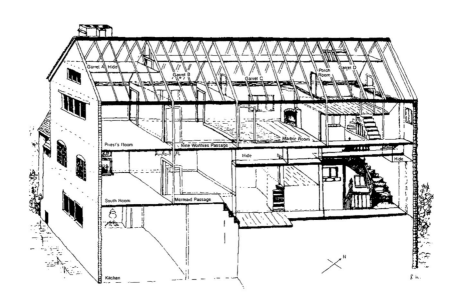

HIDDEN BRITAIN

What of the hide itself? The entrance is in the Withdrawing Room over the gateway on the first floor. To the left of the Renaissance fireplace a door opens on a short passage. A modern trapdoor lifts up to disclose a hole in the thickness of the stonework besides a fireplace, below. It is 3m deep, 1.4m by 60cm wide and has a bare earth floor. A modern, wooden ladder gives access to the hide. The original – a rare survival – is preserved in an alcove, on the other side of the fireplace.

The Withdrawing Room, Harvington Hall.

The Withdrawing Room priest hole.

The Withdrawing Room priest hole's orginal ladder – a rare survival.

Chapel

Approached via a narrow, winding staircase, the chapel was used from about 1590 until the Georgian Chapel was opened in 1743. Near the side wall, in the north-west corner, two floorboards cover a small space in which vestments and other items used at Mass were hidden.

Small secret hiding place for items used for celebrating Mass.

Lady Yate's Nursery

In the wall adjoining the Nursery there is a deep recess (the back of which is a thin lath and plaster partition), which may have allowed watchers at the windows of the Nursery to hear the service. From that side, the partition appears to be a solid part of the wall.

According to tradition, there was a narrow doorway above the door to the chapel from the Nursery, which gave access to a small hide in the gable space above. It consists of a sealed-off section of triangular space, 90cm wide at its base and 90cm high, and was probably for Mass items.

South Room

A priest hole similar to the one under the Withdrawing Room can be found under the garderobe off the South Room on the first floor (over the bread oven in the Great Kitchen). It is 1.5m deep with an insulating layer of earth at the bottom, and has an original trapdoor made of three layers of oak boards, with the top layer running the entire length of the garderobe so as not to betray its presence.

Anyone who has read Granville Squire's *Secret Hiding Places* will be confused by detailed descriptions (and diagrams) of what he called 'the pulley hide', the 'most complicated arrangement for concealment and escape which has only just been investigated'. A hole in the corner of the South Room hide was found to lead into a deep shaft from the roof to a chamber below ground level. Fastened on a bracket near the hole was a large pulley wheel. 'It is quite evident that scheme was for a person to climb through the hole and lower himself down the shaft,' wrote Squires.

The spit wheel shaft.

According to Michael Hodgetts (Harvington Hall's Historical Director), the shaft was built shortly after the priest hole fell into obsolescence. Its purpose was to house a pulley wheel and cord for driving the kitchen spit. Two of the hide's walls were pierced to allow the cord to pass through the shaft to the kitchen.

Squires' error is understandable. In this house anything seems possible, and his conclusions were coloured by the close proximity of the known hide and a tradition that the shaft led to an escape tunnel under the moat (to the Talbot Inn!).

Great Staircase
Restoration work between 1936 and 1947 included a faithful reproduction of the original Elizabethan (or early Jacobean) staircase, based on the remodelled original staircase at Coughton Court, nineteenth-century photographs, a painting, and Elizabethan decoration in the stairwell. The old staircase was not part of the original design, and there was once a floor at the level of the top landing.

The staircase appears to have been added with more than just improvements in mind, since Harvington's most ingenious priest holes (those thought to have been built by Nicholas Owen) are to be found nearby.

The first is in the staircase itself. From the top landing, five more steps lead up to the Nine Worthies Passage. The third and fourth steps up can be lifted to reveal a small secret hiding place, the back of which is formed by a brick and timber wall in which there is a squarish hole. Evidence of a bolt, along with the remains of hinges, proves that the gap was covered by an inner (and almost certainly camouflaged) secret door.

Behind the gap is a 1.5m by 1.7m, 1.8m-high secret chamber, built under the end of the Nine Worthies Passage and above the ceiling of the Butler's Pantry next to the Great Chamber. Hodgetts notes signs of a false ceiling of lath and plaster (which would have reduced the chances of it being discovered if the boards of the Nine Worthies Passage were taken up). Oak boards cover the floor of the hide, but there was formerly a rush mat – the remains of which are on display in the Nursery.

From the top landing, five more steps lead up to the Nine Worthies Passage. The third and fourth steps up can be lifted to reveal a secret hiding place.

It is said there was a spy or air hole from the hide, camouflaged by the painted frieze that covered the upper part of the Great Chamber. Since most of the frieze has disappeared and the brickwork has been repointed, it is impossible to say whether or not this is true. Another rumour maintains there was a means to pass provisions into the hide from the pantry, below.

Marble Room

Moving a short distance along the Nine Worthies Passage, we arrive at the Marble Room. This room and the two rooms beyond (one of which is called the Priest's Room) form a suite and are likely to have been the rooms used by priests. Here a triangular, brick fireplace appears blackened by the soot of centuries – but do not be deceived. There is no chimney stack on the two floors below, and the fireplace rests on the floorboards. The 'flue' provides entry to the garret above, and does not continue past the tiles. A projecting brick, just out of sight from the fireplace, provides a foothold to climb up and down the shaft. From the garret above, it appears as a roughly circular brick shaft in a corner, smoothed over with mortar so boards could be placed over it.

Large Garret Hide

The large garret hide is indirectly accessed from a curious, unnamed room at the top the Great Staircase, accessed via six steps up from the top landing, next to the steps to the Nine Worthies Passage. Hodgetts calls the unnamed room the Pilate Room and it occupies both garret space and some additional space that was created when a new ceiling was inserted at the top of the original staircase. From the Pilate Room it is possible to climb through an opening that

False fireplace in the Marble Room.

was likely a camouflaged door into a long, low roof void, 1.3m high to the apex above. Some 9m along there is a lath and plaster wall with an opening where, again, there is evidence of a lockable entrance door.

From here one can climb down into a large space above the Priest's Room, approximately 5m by 4m and 2m to the apex of the gable. It is lined with boards on the inside and old nails in the joists, indicating there was a boarded floor. 'There can be no doubt that the space was used for habitation,' says Hodgetts, 'and the absence until recently of any other entrance proves that it was a hiding place.' Evidence for this cunningly designed conversion can be seen in the Priest's Room below. Here the height of the ceiling was raised to incorporate some of the space and a window that belonged to the end garret. As a consequence, the floor level in the hide is well above the floor level of the adjacent garret room, greatly improving its security.

Dr Dodd's Library

An ingenious and delightful hide can be found in the room named after Hugh Tootell (*c.* 1671–1743), alias Charles Dodd. The Lancashire-born priest spent twenty years writing his *Church History of England* at Harvington Hall. The hide was rediscovered in 1896, illustrating how effective it was.

From the landing between the Great Chamber and the Mermaid Passage, six steps lead up into the room. At the opposite end to the window there is a 1.6m high, 1m deep platform, formerly a panelled cupboard, on which has been placed a seventeenth-century oak coffer. Upon climbing onto this platform, the

The hide in Dr Dodd's Library.

stout upright post nearest the panelled wall swings out, if pressed near the top, above its iron pivot. At the bottom, an oak stop prevents undue movement. The chamber beyond is 2.4m long, just under 1m wide and 1.5m high. It occupies difficult-to-detect space between a lowered section of ceiling in the Mermaid Passage and the floor of the Marble Room, above. Today the interior can be viewed through a window in the back of a cupboard on the newel staircase.

False Floors?

Bolt hole and tunnel traditions are inevitable in a house like this. Stories about 'false floors' are less common. Such tales must be taken with a big pinch of salt, but something similar seems to have existed at nearby Hindlip Hall (p. 179, n. 16). In a letter to Anne Vaux, the Jesuit priest Henry Garnet said, 'I found a board taken up where through was a great downfall, that one should have broken his neck had he come thither in the dark, which seemed intended for the purpose.'[56]

Fear not. Whilst Harvington's boards were unsafe prior to the hall's restoration, that certainly is not the case today!

Kidderminster DY10 4LR; Archdiocese of Birmingham, open part year.

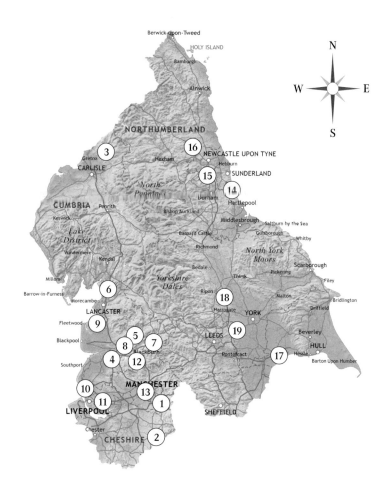

Northern England's castles, halls and manor houses are a rich repository of treasures, priest holes and other antiquities. Here you will encounter a hinged portrait, spyholes, moveable panels and secret passageways.

1. LYME PARK CHESHIRE

◇◇

It was from the lake in the park here that Mr Darcy famously emerged in the 1995 BBC adaptation of *Pride and Prejudice*. Home to the Leigh family for six centuries, Lyme Park lies on moorland at the western edge of the Peak District and is the highest stately home in England.

The Leigh family were given Lyme in 1398 for services to Richard II's father, the Black Prince, and held it until 1946 when the house was given over to the National Trust. It became the family's principal seat in the mid-sixteenth century after Sir Piers Leigh (1514–89) built the core of the present house. Venetian architect Giacomo Leoni remodelled the largely Elizabethan mansion in 1725–35. The south front is entirely Leoni, dominated by a classical portico extending the full height of the house with giant lead figures of Venus, Neptune and Pan set along the pediment.

Surviving Elizabethan interiors include the Long Gallery and a richly panelled Tudor drawing room. The gloomy, full length portrait of the Black Prince in the entrance hall is a reminder that Lyme was won for the Leigh family on the battlefields of Crécy, France in 1346.

The portrait hides a secret: it swings out on its frame. This particular example is thought to have inspired Sir Walter Scott, who used the idea in his novel *Woodstock* (1826). It opens into the drawing room, and was originally an ordinary doorframe. However, the level of the room was dropped in the eighteenth century and there was an opportunity to create an architectural curiosity. Hinges, and a cord and pulley arrangement, allow the picture to be drawn back into its place after being swung out. The floor in the drawing room is level with the bottom of the picture, and there is a concealed door that gives access to the back.

Genuine secret hiding places can be found on the top floor, in the King's Chamber. The floorboards in a closet to the right of the fireplace can be taken up over a place where stone has been removed from the wall underneath, giving access to two chambers. One, beyond the chimney, is 3.4m long, 1.2m wide and a little under 1m high. The other is the same height, but 3.4m square and occupies a space under the Knight's Chamber.

Disley SK12 2NR; National Trust, open part year, parks and gardens open all year.

2. Little Moreton Hall Cheshire

◇◇

This spectacular example of a half-timbered moated manor house seems to belong to a Brother's Grimm fairy tale. Black, white and asymmetric, it appears like a collection of house parts bolted together in a crazy, haphazard fashion. It is just as breathtaking on the inside.

An earlier moated building stood here, but construction of the present house began around 1504–08 for wealthy Cheshire landowner William Moreton, initially around three sides of a courtyard, but later to an H-plan. Its present, agglomerated appearance is the result of seven or more rebuilds. Much was added during the sixteenth century, including an additional range to the eastern wing, which included a chapel.

It is said that two small rooms in the guest's parlour on the first floor were formerly shut off from the rest of the house by a sliding panel in the north wall of the apartment over the kitchen. However, they were later used to store cheese, and the secret entrance was destroyed. The panel was 'restored' in the mid-1930s in accordance with a description in Henry Taylor's *Old Catholic Halls of Lancashire and Cheshire* (1884):

> The two secret apartments or hiding-rooms are in the little wing at the back of the gatehouse at its north-west corner. They are each about nine feet square, and in all probability served, one as the sitting-room and the other as the bedroom of the unfortunate priest or other fugitive who had to be concealed from his pursuers. The only access to these two rooms is by a sliding panel in the north wall of the apartment over the kitchen; but some pressure must have been applied to a stout priest to get him through this narrow aperture. Of such neat manufacture is the panelling that much time might be spent by the pursuer in discovering that any part of it was moveable, or that anything like a door existed in it.

Taylor goes on to describe an interesting subterranean passage:

> In the westernmost of these secret rooms is a black-looking abyss, or shaft, about four feet by three feet, and down this hole the fugitive is said to have descended to the subterranean passage under the moat. Mr. Myott, the agent of the property, informs me that this underground passage, passing under the moat, has been followed up for some distance, a chimney sweep having been employed for the purpose. This passage leads in the direction of a mound which stands not many yards from the south-west corner of the moat. I have not personally investigated the facts relating to this under-ground passage, but in the nature of things it is not improbable that such a means of escape did once exist.

Given Taylor's description, the now blocked passage is a good candidate for a drain exploited as a bolt hole.

Congleton CW12 4SD; National Trust, open part year.

3. NAWORTH CASTLE CUMBRIA

◇◇

This former stronghold of the Lord Wardens of the Marches dates to the fourteenth century. Naworth was altered during the sixteenth century by Thomas Dacre, 2nd Baron Dacre of Gisland (1467–1525) and it was he who built what became known as Lord William's Tower.

Thomas was succeeded by his only son, William Dacre, 3rd Baron Dacre of Gisland (*c.* 1500–63). Following William's death his son (another Thomas) succeeded his father as baron. However, this Lord Dacre died in 1566 leaving a widow, Elizabeth, three young daughters and a son, George. The vast Dacre estates came under the control of the Howard family when the widowed Elizabeth secretly married Queen Elizabeth I's second cousin, Thomas Howard, 4th Duke of Norfolk (1538–72). She died in childbirth in 1567 and the duke was granted wardship of her children and arranged for his sons to marry Elizabeth's three daughters. Elizabeth's 9-year-old son George (5th Baron Dacre) died in 1569 after falling from a horse.

Although Norfolk was brought up as a Protestant, his family had Roman Catholic leanings. In 1569 he was imprisoned for scheming to marry Mary, Queen of Scots, but in the end was executed for his involvement in the Ridolfi plot to assassinate Queen Elizabeth.

The eldest Dacre daughter, Elizabeth, married Norfolk's third son, Lord William Howard (1563–1640). Since his wife's estates had been seized by Queen Elizabeth, Lord William had to raise £10,000 to reclaim them. After this was achieved in 1602 he set about restoring Naworth. He was an antiquarian and reputed priest harbourer, and Lord William's Tower acquired its name after he remodelled it to accommodate his bed chamber, library and chapel.

A section of hinged panel at the side of the altar can be moved to allow a trapdoor in the floor to be opened (the device is a nineteenth-century construction, but may have been based on the original). Beneath the trapdoor, a few steps lead to a secret chamber about 1.5m square, with an additional recess in the thickness of the wall containing a discrete window slit, scarcely visible on the outside.

Brampton CA8 2HF; private house, residential and non-residential group tours by appointment.

4. Dunkirk Hall Lancashire

◇◇◇

Formerly known as Rider Hall, the home of the staunchly Roman Catholic Rider Family can be dated to 1628. Now a pub, there is a tradition that an upper room at the back of the house was used as a secret chapel and that there was a priest hole here. Indeed, a recess with steps leads up into a chimney to the right of the ground floor fireplace, behind which lies a mysterious, walled-in space.

Leyland PR26 7SW; public house.

5. STONYHURST COLLEGE LANCASHIRE

The approach is spectacular. At the end of a long drive flanked by vast orna-mental lakes, twin cupola-topped towers soar above an embattled Elizabethan gatehouse. The former seat of the Roman Catholic Shireburn family is today a famous Roman Catholic independent school adhering to the Jesuit tradition.

Dating to the 1590s, Shireburn Mansion (Stonyhurst Hall) is the oldest extant building, created when Sir Richard Shireburn (d. 1594) began remodelling and extending an earlier mansion. Although his son, another Richard (c. 1546–1629) continued with the work, it was never completed (Oliver Cromwell spent a night there in 1648, and called Stonyhurst 'a fine half house'). Stonyhurst was enlarged and aggrandised in the 1690s under Sir Nicholas Shireburn (1658–1717), the last of the family to live in the mansion. Upon his death, Shireburn possessions passed to their relatives, the Weld family of Lulworth Castle, Dorset.

Stonyhurst College is the descendant of the Jesuit college for the sons of English recusant families that was founded in 1592 by Father Robert Persons at Saint Omer in Artois, France (then part of the Spanish Netherlands). Forced to relocate twice because of the suppression of the Jesuit order (first to Bruges in 1762 and then in 1773 to Liège) the college returned to England in 1794 when Thomas Weld offered an unused Stonyhurst to the Society of Jesus.

The college's four main libraries and two museums house a fascinating collection of relics, altar furniture and prohibited literature. Occasionally dis-played is the exquisitely beautiful prayer book thought to have belonged to Mary, Queen of Scots, which she is believed to have taken to her execution, a lock of her hair, a hat that belonged to St Thomas More, the table on which an unwelcome Oliver Cromwell slept and Arthur Conan Doyle's school desk.

Stonyhurst's priest holes are mentioned in college chronicles, but there are no records of them being used (except during Jacobite times).

One was located in the Duchess' Rooms before they were pulled down to make way for the Arundel Library wing. It was hidden behind a bookcase, the back of which (allegedly) opened by touching a secret spring. When found, it contained a bed and some guineas from the period of James II. Another, smaller hide, was found in a hollow beam and contained an old towel and the skull of a rat. The third was found nearby, beneath a flagstone in the original washing place.

Stonyhurst's collection includes a set of Jacobite long pistols, their butts weighted with lead so that after discharging they could be used as clubs. They were found, together with a flask of rum, in a still extant hide located up a false chimney in the gatehouse (behind a carved marble shield bearing the Shireburn arms). Another extant hide is located over the Long Room, entered via a trapdoor under a window seat in the room above. It is 3.2m long, 1m at its widest point and just 76cm deep.

Clitheroe BB7 9PZ; Catholic co-educational independent boarding
and day school, open part year for weekend tours, gardens also open
weekends.

6. Borwick Hall Lancashire

◇◇

Incorporating fourteenth-century remains, this gabled and embattled
manor house was built in the late sixteenth century for wealthy clothier, Roger Bindloss. Roger's great grandson, the Anglican MP Sir Robert
Bindloss (1624–88), appears to have had Royalist sympathies but officially
supported the Parliamentarian cause during the Civil War. Wisely, he was
absent when Charles II was accommodated at Borwick Hall during his
Worcester campaign.

During the Jacobite Rebellion of 1715, Ralph Standish of Borwick Hall supported the Jacobite and Catholic cause, and Borwick's traditional hiding
place may have been linked to the concealment of arms and equipment. The
chamber (known as the 'Priest's Hiding Place') is located below the former
Protestant chapel and the chaplain's room, and was made by lowering the
ceiling of the ground floor room.

It is a shallow space, 1.5m deep between the ground and first floors and
extends the full width and breadth of the east wing. It is now entered through
a modern trapdoor from the room above (it is said that the original, pivoting
trapdoor became rotten and was replaced).

There is no evidence that the space was a priest hole but it may well have
been used as a place of concealment, even if its origins were, as some have
suggested, a cosmetic necessity to maintain the level of the floors without
increasing the height of the rooms below.

Carnforth LA6 1JU; residential outdoor education and conference
centre, open all year other than Christmas period.

7. Towneley Hall Lancashire

◇◇

Now a museum, Towneley had a remarkable series of priest holes. It was first
mentioned in a deed of about 1200 when the Norman baron Roger de Lacy
made a grant of 'two bovates' (30–40 acres) of land for a new hunting lodge
in 'Tunlea' to Geoffrey, the son of Robert, Dean of Whalley.

The present building was begun around 1400 and had a great hall and two
wings. Later, in the time of Elizabeth I, it was a courtyard house with a fourth

Borwick Hall.

wing forming a quadrangle, but this was demolished in the early eighteenth century. Little of the original structure survives, except a rubble wall on the courtyard side of the south-east wing. Some 1.8m thick, it contains a mysterious spiral staircase not shown on plans.

There was a chapel here as early as the thirteenth century – probably in the woods behind the hall. In Elizabethan times, it was located in the fourth wing and had a library over it (though, as we have seen, this fourth wing was demolished). The chapel, along with its panelled oak door, wainscot and other artefacts were moved to their present location in the north-west corner of the house. The beautiful, 26m Long Gallery is situated on the upper floor of the fifteenth-century south wing, though internally, the wing has been much altered over the years.

The Towneleys of Towneley Hall were an ancient family, able to trace their ancestry to the deans of Whalley. Lancashire was a hotbed of recusancy during the Elizabethan period and the family was marked down on Lord Burleigh's list of recusants as 'of more than ordinary perversity'. Indeed, John Towneley (1528–1607) suffered imprisonment and heavy fines for his adherence to the old faith. In 1558 he was tried and arrested at Lathom Hall and admitted to giving shelter to a former Catholic priest. Later, leading members of the family supported the Jacobite Rebellions and Francis Towneley (1709–46) was executed for his role in the rebellion of 1745.

At one time there were eight priest holes at Towneley, all listed in an untraced early eighteenth-century document that was quoted in F. Odo Blundell's *Old Catholic Lancashire*:

A Note of the Private Places at Towneley
The Library
In the library over against the closet door the middle panel slides back, and the same over against the window. On the floor over against the door, the base slides up and takes out; in the floor is a hole, in which an iron hook is to be put, and will open to a large place by lifting up the whole floor. At the back side of the library door, the side wainscote may be taken out, and lets you into a place, where some boards may be taken up, which will let you into a large place, which held all the library books.

The Chapel
At the chapel door taking up one board, which is not nailed fast, will let you into such another. In the chapel the alter [*sic*] table draws out, and also the upper steps, which will let you into a large place, in which may be laid all the gilding, which is only put on with pegs and takes to pieces; care must be taken not to knock the gilding in taking down or putting up.

Over the canopy of the alter in the library lies a door for the tabernacle, balls for the top of the pillars, instead of the flower pots, and also capitals and bottoms instead of the gilding, so that the place may be made use of though the gilding be taken down.

The Staircase
At the steps going from the stone stairs to the garret a step may be taken out, where there is a large place all over the green parlour.

The Long Gallery
In the second room in the gallery the wainscoting opens in the middle of the chimney upon hinges, where there is a hole in the wall not very big. In the third room in the gallery is the close stool closet, the panel towards the garden has a latch within, which is opened with an iron pin at a hole in the door, which lifts up the latch, which may be made faster by those within: it has a seat and will hold two persons.

When Squires visited he made several errors in relation to the chapel and the library, apparently seeing evidence for hiding places but, as mentioned previously, both the chapel and library were in the (by then) demolished gatehouse.

Of the eight priest holes, the only confirmed survival is above the Green Parlour off the Great Hall. This secret chamber is one of the largest known, 5.5m by 4.6m and tall enough to walk upright inside it. It takes up space from the loft of the Green Parlour, below it. The floor is covered in a layer of sound-deadening clay and there were once four air holes (pointed over on the outside). The original stone stairs had a moveable step like the one at Harvington Hall, but have since been renewed and the way in is now a modern trapdoor over a small landing. The parlour and staircase and the back wall of this part of the hall were reconstructed in 1725, but the hide was retained. Why? As Jacobites, perhaps the Towneleys thought it might again prove useful.

The atmospheric Long Gallery is lined with Tudor panelling and hung with weapons and trophies. In the rooms leading off it the panelling (wainscoting) is of various dates and the hide in the second room appears lost. Squires pointed out a door in the Queen Anne panelling of the third room, behind which there is a closet he thought was the hide described.

Burnley BB11 3RQ; museum, open all year, closed Fridays.

8. SAMLESBURY HALL LANCASHIRE

◇◇

This fine black and white house was the seat of the Southworth family and a noted resort of priests. They included Edmund Campion, who stayed here during Easter in 1581, a few months before he was captured and executed.

Dating to the fifteenth century but much altered, Samlesbury was originally built of timber around three sides of a courtyard. It had a moat and, prior to construction of the A677, was particularly secluded. Only the west and south wings remain. With the exception of a few uprights, the wonderful external timber work is modern.

Between a room projecting above a large, hexagonal bay window at the inner angle of the two wings and the roof of the Great Hall there is a priest hole capable of holding several men. Its position corresponds to a description of a place found during a raid in November 1592, 'a secret vault over the dining chamber'. The little room adjoining it once had bloodstains on the floor, the story being that a priest was dragged from the hole and murdered there. Another priest hole at the side of the chimney in the entrance hall was partly blocked up and its secret entrance destroyed during alterations. The same chimney stack was believed to contain yet another hide, said to have received air from an ornamental ventilating brick that is visible on the outer wall.

The interest continues. In addition to priest holes, Samlesbury has a 'secret passageway'. It was found to be 1.2m high with brick lining and was entered through a vault near the entrance hall fireplace. Both ends run towards the now dry moat, and it was originally a drain. However, given the hall's history and the nearby priest holes, it might well have had alternative uses.

Preston PR5 0UP; Samlesbury Hall Trust, open all year, closed Saturdays.

9. Thurnham Hall Lancashire

<><><><><><><><><><><><><><><><><><><><><><><><><><><><><><><><><><><><><><>

The de Thurnhams were the earliest possessors of this venerable estate, which passed by descent to various families of note, including the Greys. Thomas Grey, 1st Marquess of Dorset (1455–1501) was the eldest son of Elizabeth Woodville and Sir John Grey of Groby. Elizabeth was an ambitious beauty of middle-ranking status. Her second marriage to King Edward IV in 1464 was the sensation of the day.

Grey fought at the Battle of Tewkesbury and later took arms against Richard III, joining Buckingham's failed rebellion of 1483. He fled to Brittany, joining Henry Tudor there. Two years later, on 22 August 1485, Henry took the crown at the Battle of Bosworth Field. However, the new king did not trust Grey and had him imprisoned during the Pretender Lambert Simnel's rising in 1487. His estates, including Thurnham, were forfeited to the crown until after the House of Tudor victory at the Battle of Stoke Field in June 1487.

Grey's great granddaughter, Lady Jane Grey (c. 1537–54), 'The Nine Days' Queen', was executed on the orders of Mary I. Her father, the 3rd Marquess, sold the Thurnham estate to a London grocer called Thomas Lonne, who in 1556 sold it to the Roman Catholic Robert Dalton of Bispham (d. 1615), also in Lancashire. Dalton, a relative of the Towneleys of Towneley (p. 123) is thought to have erected the present three-storey house in the latter half of the sixteenth century, on and incorporating earlier fabric. Through marriage, Thurnham passed to the de Hoghtons, a Roman Catholic family with pro-Royalist and Jacobite sympathies.

Now a hotel, Thurnham's nineteenth-century pseudo-gothic façade of corner turrets and embattled parapet is said to have replaced a front with three gables, an embattled porch and mullioned windows. The Great Hall still boasts oak panelling, a magnificent Tudor fireplace and armorial stained-glass windows. A warren of stone Jacobean staircases, galleries and bedrooms terminate at the ancient pele tower. There is also a beautiful private chapel (not the old secret chapel). This one was paid for by Elizabeth Dalton – the last lineal member of the family bearing the name Dalton – and was built in 1854.

Located on the first floor, a bedroom apartment (Room 6) is the traditional haunt of a lady in green. Her appearance is said to herald impending danger – so it is fitting that there is a priest hole off it. Remarkably well preserved, it is located at the back of the chimney of the Tudor fireplace.

To the left of the fireplace, a narrow stone doorway opens into a windowless stone-floored space (now the apartment kitchen). At the far end, on the left, there is a large stone missing, behind which is a small hide with a stone seat in the thickness of the stack. It is around 1.8m high, about 1m deep and a little over 0.5m wide. The missing stone was kept at Lancaster Old Town Hall, but has now been returned. The inside was left rough but the outside was faced to blend in with the wall. This is an important and rare survival (perhaps the only example in England), for the stone was hinged and could be opened.

Iron bars driven into its thickness allowed this, and the remains of the L-shaped pins that supported the bars are still present. The upper bar is still attached to its pin. There was a similar device at Longhorsley Tower, 10km north of Morpeth.

In the wall opposite the hide another, much smaller stone slides, out to reveal a small cavity that may have been used to hide valuables or incriminating items.

Thurnham LA2 0DT; country house hotel, conference and events venue.

10. Lydiate Hall Merseyside

◇◇◇

After falling into disrepair in the first half of the twentieth century, Lydiate Hall became a romantic woodland ruin.

The hall was a typical two-storey half-timbered, sixteenth-century house, originally built around four sides of a small courtyard and with an exterior of panelling and bands of quatrefoils of white plaster set in black wood (reminiscent of Speke Hall, below). Since this was the seat of the Roman Catholic Ireland family (often in trouble for recusancy), several priest holes were constructed here.

One was found in 1841 in the chimney adjoining the chapel, which contained the leg bone of a chicken. Another was found amidst the rafters.

To the south of the old hall are the remains of the Ireland's private chapel, called Lydiate Abbey and dedicated to St Catherine. According to tradition, a secret tunnel ran between the two buildings.

Lydiate, Liverpool L31 4HD; the fourteenth-century Scotch Piper Inn provides a good base from which to explore the remains of the chapel and the public footpaths around the hall. The hall's outbuildings house a farm shop.

11. Speke Hall Merseyside

A riot of black and white, this magical, half-timbered manor house was the seat of the Roman Catholic Norris family. Occupying an old moated site on the banks of the River Mersey, the present building was constructed on a sandstone base around four sides of a cobbled courtyard. Nineteenth-century restoration resulted in what the National Trust describes as 'a unique and beautiful mixture of Tudor simplicity and Victorian Arts and Crafts aesthetics'.

The T-shaped Great Hall rises to the roof and is suitably adorned with carvings, antlers, paintings and suits of armour. At its western end, the 'Great Wainscot' incorporates fine pilasters and Flemish Renaissance-style carved heads. In the Great Parlour next door, panels in the early Jacobean plaster ceiling depict a profusion of fruits, vines and roses.

Speke was likely begun by Sir William Norris (d. 1506) and was subjected to extensive remodelling in about 1530 by his grandson, another Sir William (1501–68). In 1598, the latter's eldest surviving son, Edward, built the north wing and equipped it with priest holes. In 1598, it was reported that two priests known as 'Little Sir Richard' and 'Sir Peter' spent most of their time 'lodged in a chamber over the parlour'.[57]

The larger of two known priest holes lies over cupboards and behind the upper part of the panelling to the right of the fireplace in the Green Room. Access is via a panelled closet door to the left of the fireplace, where a modern ladder give access to a 2m square, 1.5m-high space between the chimney breast and the Green Room panelling. The hide can be indirectly reached from above, via a modern trapdoor in the attic, next to the chimney stack.

The other, slightly smaller priest hole can be found nearby, next to the Tapestry Room above the gateway (also called the Haunted Room, since it is reputedly haunted by Mary Norris, the last heiress of the Norris family). Like the other hide it has two approaches: either through another trapdoor in the attic or through a modern plaster-covered door above the door of the cupboard in the dressing room next to the Tapestry Room.

To complement Speke's priest holes, a spyhole in the Blue Bedroom gives a view of the main approach to the house and there is an original 'eavesdrop', over the courtyard entrance to the screens. The small hole made it possible to hear the conversations of people awaiting admission.

Liverpool L24 1XD; National Trust, open part year, variable opening times.

12. Hall i' th' Wood Greater Manchester

〈〈

The appearance and history of this sixteenth-century, timber-framed house lives up to its intriguing name. It is a reference in the local dialect, pronounced 'Hallith Wood', and the fact that the house was erected amidst the ancient oak woodland that once dominated the local countryside. It has the distinction of being the house where in 1779 Samuel Compton, whose family rented part of it, perfected his spinning mule.

Now a museum, when architectural historian Nikolaus Pevsner visited he described its present situation as, 'An uninviting approach through modern housing, a bleak playing field, a sudden vision of decorative sixteenth-century timber framing and seventeenth-century stone mullions and pinnacles, and an unsuspected river valley, steep and wooded.'

The building has two storeys, attics and a stone roof. The oldest part, built in the mid-sixteenth century by wealthy local landowner Lawrence Brownlow, consists of the usual arrangement of great hall, standing north to south, with the now absent screens and passage at the lower end.

The house reputedly has hiding places, with various spaces that could have been adapted for concealment. Crompton is said to have been forced to dismantle his spinning mule and hide the parts in a 'priest hole' during local machine-breaking riots in the nineteenth century.

According to writer Fletcher Moss, the location of the priest hole was behind the chimney of the Crompton Room, though as Squires notes, there is no hiding place there. There is, however, a long narrow hole over the adjoining stair that can be reached from the garrets. Another (more likely) candidate is a 3m long, 1.5m high space in the north wing that can be reached via a hole in the ceiling east of the kitchen. It is probably an 'architectural space', never intended to hide anything – but put to good use when the need arose.

Bolton BL1 8UA; museum, limited opening part year.

13. Bramall Hall Greater Manchester

〈〈

This delightful black and white timber-framed manor house dates to the fourteenth century (with the usual sixteenth- and nineteenth-century additions), and was built for Alice and John Davenport. The Davenports held the manor for five centuries.

Originally a courtyard house, the building is illustrative of timber framing techniques from the mid-fifteenth to the late sixteenth centuries. However, the west wing was demolished around 1774 to leave the current, U-shaped ground plan.

Bramall Hall is said to have a hiding place that harboured a Cavalier (the Davenports were Royalists). It can be found behind a panelled door on the left side of the fireplace in what was called the 'Ghost Room' (Paradise Room), north of the Nevill Room (also called the Chapel, Priest's or Queen Anne Room). It appears to be a small recess – perhaps a closet or garderobe – but in times past it was said to be an open passage leading to a secret chamber between the Nevill Room floor and the Chapel below. Squires maintained that there was an entrance 'made later from a modern room constructed in the upper portion of the lofty chapel'. However, he was referring to a blocked-up doorway by the side of the fireplace in the Chapel Room that was probably a door made redundant following late sixteenth- and early seventeenth-century restructuring of the wing.

Long thought to be haunted, the atmospheric Paradise Room is named after the former early seventeenth-century bed hangings depicting Adam and Eve's Fall that hung here, embroidered by Dorothy Davenport, wife of Sir William Davenport (c.1563–1639), now in Capesthorne Hall, Cheshire.

Stockport SK7 3NX; museum, open all year.

14. HARDWICK HALL COUNTY DURHAM

Hardwick Hall hides a secret: this plain, early to mid-eighteenth-century country house contains an Elizabethan core. The Maire family held Hardwick for many years and were serial recusants, beginning in 1590 when the then Protestant Robert Maire and his wife, Grace (the daughter of a wealthy Puritan lawyer), witnessed the execution of four young priests in Durham. They were so moved by the display of faith and courage, they converted.

Traces of a chapel can be found at the top of the house, and in a garret above there is an interesting priest hole. Reached via a ceiling trapdoor, a large chimney breast conceals an addition that in fact takes up most of the observed chimney. It is difficult to detect in low light, and a hammer-wielding priest hunter would *expect* to hear a hollow ring. A false wall that conceals the space is supported by the floorboards only; a fact concealed by a ridge of mortar around the base.

The hide itself is high enough to stand up in, 0.5m long and just over 1m wide. It has a wooden seat and a head-high shelf (both attached to the real chimney) and is entered via a full-size wooden door in a dark corner, under the sloping roof. The door opens inwards and has been camouflaged with a thick coat of painted plaster that looks and feels like brickwork, though it was probably refurbished during the eighteenth century. It was secured by way of the remarkably intact rough iron bolt.

The same renovations that led to the hide's discovery revealed an ancient staircase that was perhaps converted to secrecy. It has been opened up and leads close to the room below the garret hide.

In a thickly wooded dingle near to the hall is a brook called the Hardwick Deene. About 400m downstream there is an artificial cave in the left bank of a sandstone cliff. A little under 3m deep and 2m wide, the cave was used as a hideout cum secret chapel, and had a crucifix set in the wall.

Hardwick Hall (Hardwicke Hall Manor) Hesleden Road, Blackhall Colliery, Hartlepool TS27 4PA; country house hotel.

15. LORD CREWE ARMS NORTHUMBERLAND

W.H. Auden stayed here at Easter 1930. He later said, 'it is a number of years now since I stayed at the Lord Crewe Arms, but no other spot brings me sweeter memories.' The inn occupies former ancillary buildings associated with Blanchland Abbey and, though subjected to extensive remodelling during the eighteenth century, it retains a hotchpotch of ancient fabric.

In the huge kitchen chimney, visitors may view the famous 'Priest's Hole'. However, given its location, and the fact that a large fire would be needed to deter the immediate discovery of any priest foolish enough to hide inside, it was probably a chamber for smoking and preserving foods.

Blanchland, Consett DH8 9SP; country house hotel.

16. CAPHEATON HALL NORTHUMBERLAND

This Grade I listed Jacobean house was built by Robert Trollope in 1668 for the Roman Catholic Royalist Sir John Swinburne, 1st Baronet (d. 1706). It remains the home of the Swinburne family (now Browne-Swinburne) and contained some of the latest priest holes on record.

There were two in the chapel at the top of the house, one of which was closed by a picture above the altar that pivoted to reveal a way into a roof space. A hide behind a chimney was accessed from the roof via a slate-covered shaft and had an interesting story attached to it.

A prominent Jacobite leader during the Fifteen (uprising in 1715), James Radcliffe, 3rd Earl of Derwentwater (1689–1716) was beheaded on Tower Hill after being taken at the Battle of Preston (1715). Before the battle, Derwentwater had arranged for his servants to remove important papers from his seat at Dilston Hall and take them to Capheaton (the families were connected through marriage). Thirty years after his death they were found by a Presbyterian slater named Walton. He reported the find to the authorities, the property was searched and the papers recovered. As a consequence, the Crown was able to seize the Dilston estates.

A possible hide under the floor of a closet on the first floor landing still exists. Though closed up, it is said to run between the floors of the house and to have an exit into the grounds via a shaft and a short tunnel. There's another hide beneath a closet leading out of a bedroom on the same floor. Its trapdoor has been replaced, but a hole in the wood for the old bolt is still visible in the supporting beam. It is about 1.5m high, a little under 3m long and a little over 1m wide. A rough brick wall separates the hide from the rest of the space below the bedroom floor.

Capheaton, Newcastle upon Tyne NE19 2AB; private house with accommodation, group tours by written appointment.

17. CARLTON TOWERS YORKSHIRE

With a mass of turrets, gargoyles and battlements, the present L-shaped house is the epitome of Victorian extravagance. However, the interior of the three-storey, square-shaped block is clearly much older and incorporates the Carlton Hall of 1614.

Here was the seat of the Roman Catholic Stapleton family, whose distinguished ancestors held the Manor of Carlton from the time of the Norman Conquest and for centuries afterward. Within the old part of the house (which was, for a time, a Jesuit chaplaincy) there is a Jacobean-era priest hole. The entrance is through a trapdoor in a large fireside closet in the 'Priest's Hiding Hole Room' on the top floor.

A modern ladder leads down into a secret chamber next to a huge chimney stack (visible through glass floor panels). It measures approximately 4m by 2.5m and a little less than 2m high.

Carlton DN14 9LZ; private house, accommodation, conference and events venue.

18. RIPLEY CASTLE YORKSHIRE

◇◇

For seven centuries Ripley Castle has been the seat of the Ingilby family, whose boar head crest commemorates the time in 1355 when Sir Thomas Ingilby (1310–69 saved Edward III from a wild boar. The gatehouse was built in the 1450s by Sir John Ingilby, and Sir William (1518–78) completed the Old Tower in about 1555, containing the Library, Tower Room and Knight's Chamber. The old manor house fell into disrepair after a serious fire in 1761 and the main house was rebuilt in the 1780s, attached to the Old Tower. The coach house and stable block were completed at the beginning of the 1800s. Today, this stands as the east wing of the castle (restored in 2004 as a banqueting facility).

The Ingilbys were prominent recusants as well as Royalists during the Civil War. Their history is colourful to say the least. In 1603 Sir William Ingleby (1546–1618) played host to James VI of Scotland en route to the king's coronation as James I of England but within two years he was implicated in a plot to kill the king, his family and hundreds of MPs. In fact, the Ingilbys were related to or closely associated with nine of the eleven principal Gunpowder Plot conspirators (the mother of Robert and Thomas Wyntour, two of the leading conspirators, was an Ingilby). Fortunately for Sir William, there was little by way of hard evidence. The trial collapsed and he was acquitted.

Sir William Ingilby (1594–1652) fought at the Battle of Marston Moor (1644) alongside his 43-year-old sister, 'Trooper' Jane Ingilby (she was disguised as a man). The king's army was routed, but Sir William and Jane managed to get back to Ripley Castle. According to an oft-repeated (and unconfirmed) tradition, they were followed by Oliver Cromwell himself, who at that time was an ambitious Lieutenant General of horse under supreme Parliamentarian commander, Edward Montagu, 2nd Earl of Manchester.

Sir William hid, perhaps in an old priest hole, leaving his sister to deal with Cromwell and his men. After long negotiation Cromwell alone was let in but held hostage at gunpoint in the library to prevent him from searching the house. The following morning he was forcefully escorted to the door – and he chose not to return.

For a long time it was assumed that Ripley has undiscovered priest holes, perhaps connected to the activities of Francis Ingilby (b. c.1551) following his ordination as a Seminary Jesuit Priest in 1583. Francis, described as 'short but well-made, fair-complexioned, with a chestnut beard, and a slight cast in his eyes'[58] was sentenced to be hung, drawn and quartered at Knavesmere, York in 1586. Upon hearing this, he said, 'Credo videre bona Domini in terra viventium' (I believe to see the good things of our Lord: in the land of the living) and whilst being shackled at the prison door, said smilingly, 'I fear me I shall be overproud of my new boots' (meaning his shackles).

By tradition, a priest hole was said to be located near the large chimney in the present library, which contains old portraits and is richly panelled. Whilst undergoing treatment for woodworm and dry rot in 1964, a priest hole was found at the top of the Old Tower in the dimly lit Knight's Chamber. Essentially unchanged for 450 years, the room contains the finest portraits in the house, boasts an original oak ceiling and contains a collection of old armour and weapons. In addition, Cromwellian-era boots and shoes are kept here.

The Knight's Chamber retains its original panelling, with each panel made up of four or five wide planks. In one panel near a spiral staircase, the two right-hand planks move on internal hinges to create a secret door, behind which, in the frame, are the remains of catch holes. The hide itself is around 0.5m long, 1m wide and 1.5m high. It has a seat and a small air hole through the outside wall.

This, it seems, was an early priest hole occupying a space between the internal and external walls and the staircase. Although it would not have stood up to a search using hammers and probes, the fact that it remained hidden long after it was in use is a testament to its camouflage.

Ripley, Harrogate HG3 3AY; private house, restricted opening all year.

19. HAZELWOOD CASTLE YORKSHIRE

Hazelwood Castle.

The 'secret door'.

Hazelwood was the seat of the Vavasours, a Roman Catholic family whose ancestors were counted among the companions of William the Conqueror. The castle has late thirteenth-century origins with later alterations, including a fifteenth-century pele tower and a mid-eighteenth-century interior attributed to the famous York architect John Carr (1723–1807). The main façade is a Georgian refacing of the medieval Great Hall. Between 1967 and 1996 the castle served as a Carmelite monastery retreat.

If there were secret hiding places here they have either been lost to alterations or forgotten: Squires noted a mysterious long slab of stone in the cellars that gave a hollow ring when stamped upon. Perhaps the persistent reports of ghostly monks and disappearing priests offer a clue in this respect. However, even if you do not discover anything you will be consoled by the library's 'secret' bookcase door!

Of course, the oft-repeated story about an underground passage to Cross Roads Farm (1.5km to the north-west) can be dismissed out of hand – though there might well be old drains here.

Hazlewood LS24 9NJ; country house hotel, conference and events venue, tour packages available.

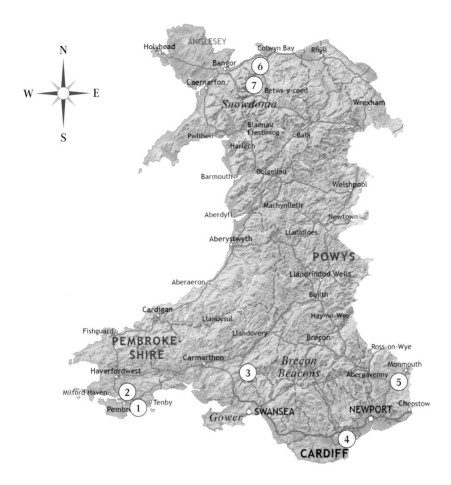

Myth and legend surrounds the castles, mansions and manor houses of Wales and they do not give up secrets easily. Look closely, and you will discover real antiquities and evidence of a hidden, cloak-and-dagger past.

1. Manorbier Castle Pembrokeshire

◇◇

Overlooking the beautiful Manorbier Beach, eleventh-century Manorbier Castle was the birthplace of the medieval chronicler and clergyman Geraldus de Barri (Gerald of Wales). He called it 'the pleasantest place in Wales'. Few will disagree.

Gerald was the great-grandson of the powerful Norman Knight Odo de Barri, who was granted the site after helping to conquer Pembrokeshire. Gerald's mother, Angharrad, was the daughter of the Welsh princess Nesta of Deheubarth, a renowned beauty and known as 'Helen of Wales'.

A visible, rectangular recess near the bottom of the castle well has long been rumoured to be a secret smuggler's passage – but it is probably a water conduit. To the south-west of the site is the medieval house, consisting of a three-storey hall built in about the twelfth century, and two later wings. There are three barrel-vaulted, windowless undercrofts beneath the hall block, two of which were sealed and left unused.

There is every reason to believe that the castle was used by smugglers for storing their contraband goods, as is the tradition in these parts. An early nineteenth century visitor recorded that the castle had been 'appropriated to smuggling, on a most daring scale. The person concerned having hired the castle of the farmer ... used to fill the subterranean apartments and towers with spirits.'[59]

Manorbier, Wales, Tenby SA70 7SY; private castle open to the public, seasonal and variable opening. Cottage accommodation is available within the castle grounds.

2. Pembroke Castle Pembrokeshire

Standing at the western fringes of the walled medieval town, Pembroke Castle was the birthplace of Henry VII. Built upon the site of an earth and timber fort, it was transformed into a mighty medieval fortress by the renowned Anglo-Norman warrior William Marshall (1147–1249) after he acquired the earldom through marriage.

The castle boasts a delightful labyrinth of passages and stairways and contains a natural limestone cave known as Wogan's Cavern. The vast, dungeon-like space was used as a storehouse or boathouse. It is 21m long and 15m wide, and is reached via a spiral staircase.

Pembroke SA71 4LA; Pembroke Castle Trust, open all year.

3. Carreg Cennan Castle Carmarthenshire

On a windswept limestone cliff stand the remains of one of Wales' most evocative castles. This large and powerful fortress has Welsh origins and was probably built by Rhys ap Gruffydd (1132–97), ruler of the kingdom of Deheubarth in South Wales. However, most of the visible stonework is English, after the castle was rebuilt after 1283 by a staunch 'king's man', the nobleman-soldier John Giffard of Brimpsfield, Gloucester and his son, also called John. The elder Giffard held the castle until his death in1299, except during the uprising of Rhys ap Maredudd in 1287–89, when it was appropriated by the Crown.

John Giffard II was executed for playing a part in a baronial uprising in 1321 against Edward II's favourite, Hugh le Despencer, and for a short time the castle passed into le Despencer hands. It again passed to the Crown via John of Gaunt, 1st Duke of Lancaster (1340–99).

Damage related to Owain Glyndwr's uprising of 1403 was repaired between 1414 and 1421 at a cost of £500 and further repairs were undertaken during the Wars of the Roses (when it was garrisoned for a time by Lancastrian supporter Grufudd ap Nicholas). However, after the Yorkist's success at the Battle of Towton (1461) much of the castle was dismantled.

A sign over a doorway in the south-east corner says 'Rhodfa i'r ogof/ Passage to cave'. Steps lead through the base of the south buttress and the south turret into a long, slit-windowed, barrel-vaulted passage along the edge of the cliff to the mouth of a dank, dark cave. It appears to have been

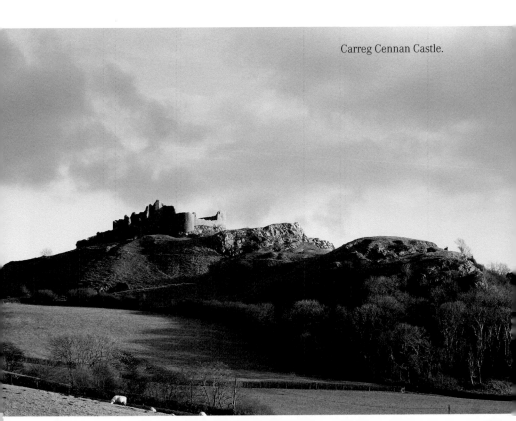

Carreg Cennan Castle.

Arrow slit in castle wall.

Barrel-vaulted passage leading down to the cave.

Cave interior, Carreg Cennan Castle.

walled off from the outside world in the thirteenth century and the wall itself contains pigeon holes. It is likely the passage and wall were created to defend a weak spot that could have been used to undermine parts of the castle.

Archaeologists have found evidence of prehistoric use of the cave, and in the nineteenth century a small quantity of Roman coins (along with a coin of Elizabeth I) were found here.

Trapp, Llandeilo SA19 6UA; private castle, open all year.

4. CARDIFF CASTLE CARDIFF

The Roman walls and medieval fortifications are fascinating. However, it is the opulent Gothic Revival mansion and eerie wall tunnels that make Cardiff a must-visit castle. The tunnels were dug under the outer walls during the Second World War and served as bomb shelters with a capacity of up to 1,800 people.

Secret tunnel rumours have a basis in fact. One was said to communicate with the wine cellar of the old Cardiff Arms (on the site of the Angel Hotel) and, in 1856, drainage contractors discovered a 1.5 metre high by 1.2m-wide masonry tunnel between the pub and the castle's west wall. Meanwhile, the eagle-eyed might spot an entry to a barrel-vaulted drain beside the Dock Feeder Canal where it runs between the castle and the New Theatre. Located near the site of the monastic settlement of Greyfriars, it could well be medieval in origin.

Cardiff CF10 3RB; museum, open all year.

5. TREOWEN COURT MONMOUTHSHIRE

Architectural historian Nikolaus Pevsner described Treowen as 'the most important early seventeenth-century gentry house in the county'. Both elegant and imposing, this stately pile boasts one of the best-preserved priest holes in Wales.

The first recorded owner of the manor of Treowen was Sir Peter Huntley after he was granted the estate for his part in the Conquest. The present house was built in the early seventeenth century and was the home of Sir Philip Jones (1602–60), who married Elizabeth Morgan of Llantarnam, a close relative of the wealthy and powerful Somerset family, earls of Worcester (of Raglan Castle).

The Morgans of Llantarnam and the earls of Worcester were leading Monmouthshire Catholics. The Somersets allowed Robert Jones, later the

TUNNELS

In his 1587 work, *The Worthiness of Wales*, Thomas Churchyard made a curious observation at the former Roman legionary fortress in Caerleon, South Wales, 'I have seen caves underground, at this day, that goe I know not how farre, all made of excellent work, and goodly greate stones, both over head and under foot, and close and fine round about the whole cave.'

To what was he referring? A main drain – this time Roman – and almost certainly associated with the baths complex (a visit will leave you in no doubt). What follows, however, is more perplexing.

Located on private land but visible over the surrounding walls, Caerleon Castle Mynde resembles a huge tree-covered Christmas pudding and is associated with local Arthurian folklore. The remains of a Norman motte and bailey, it is 65m in diameter and 30m tall.

In the early 1800s, a young man was riding around the Mynde when he noticed a small landslip that had revealed an iron door and several steps leading down to it. Strangely, his master instructed him to cover it up, which he duly did with turf and wooden pegs. Having been told this incredible tale, in 1878 the owner of the property, a Mr Robert F. Woollett, decided to drive a tunnel into the mound with the help of the man who found it – by now very old. He reported his findings to the Caerleon Antiquarian Association. Having failed to pinpoint the exact location, the pair tunnelled into the earth in its general vicinity. They found Roman pottery and tiles as well as wild boar tusks. Once 8m into the mound, they reached a mysterious wall indicating an internal structure or (more likely) the foundations of a stone building. The wall continued until at 15m they abandoned the endeavour. The question remains: what lay behind the door?

Another mystery door was associated with Tresilian Cave, between Llantwit Major and St Donat's in the Vale of Glamorgan. There was an alleged secret smuggler's passage to St Donat's Castle on the west side of the cavern. In the late nineteenth century, an elderly gentleman told Glamorgan historian Marianne Robertson Spencer that he could remember the entrance being closed by an iron door that was washed away during a storm.

Treowen Court.

Jesuit superior, to use Raglan Castle as a base, before offering a more permanent settlement at Cwm, in the parish of Llanrothal (Herefordshire).

The only date – 1627 – can be found on a carved oak passage screen in the banqueting hall. However, it is probable that this screen and porch were slightly later additions, since they are more ornate than the rest of the building. There is also an oak-panelled room with a plaster ceiling, a Jacobean fireplace and a superb, full-height Jacobean staircase.

On the first floor, just outside the door of the Tudor Rose Room, there is a modern trapdoor and ladder to a 1.8m by 1.5m, 1.4m-high lath and plaster hide under the corridor floor. In it was discovered a picture of St Mary Magdalen, on a piece of seventeenth-century parchment.

Wonastow, Monmouth NP25 4DL; private house, available for hire as a holiday home and wedding venue.

6. PLAS MAWR CONWY
◇◇◇

With its early crow-stepped gables and innovative lavish plasterwork, Plas Mawr is the most complete large Elizabethan town house in Wales. It was built for wealthy merchant Robert Wynn between 1576 and approximately 1585, erasing all traces of an older building.

Mystery meets history here: a tragic legend is supported by a genuine secret hiding place. Many years ago, the pregnant mistress of the house eagerly

Top: Treowen. A modern trapdoor leads to the priest hole. Bottom: Priest hole interior.

awaited the return of her husband, who had been away at war. For hours, she kept vigil with her 3-year-old daughter at the top floor of the tower, where she would see her husband's approach. Night came, and she grew tired of waiting. She picked up her daughter and descended the awkward spiral stairs. Suddenly, she slipped and tumbled down, seriously injuring both herself and her child. A housekeeper found the pair, summoned a doctor and had them taken to the Lantern Room.

The usual doctor was out, so his assistant, Dr Dick, was sent. Dr Dick found the mistress and the child on the verge of death. Alarmed by the situation, he told the housekeeper that he wanted to fetch the older, more experienced doctor at once.

Understandably, she would not let him leave and pushed him back into the room, saying that she would send a servant to fetch the old doctor. The housekeeper fastened the heavy door behind her.

The servant was duly dispatched. However, he could not find the old doctor and, fearful of repercussions, was not seen again for a number of years. Meanwhile the housekeeper was expecting the old doctor but, of course, he did not arrive. Eventually, the moans from the locked room faded away.

Just then, the master arrived home. The housekeeper tried as best she could to explain what had happened. He pushed past her and entered the room. The windows were fastened against a raging storm whilst dying embers smouldered in the hearth. His wife's lifeless body was on the bed, the young child's by the window. By the fireplace lay a tiny, prematurely born infant. Dr Dick was nowhere to be seen.

The master screamed at the housekeeper, 'Who has been here?' To which she replied, 'Dr Dick ... he is somewhere in this room.' The master vowed to find him. He pushed the housekeeper out of the room and slammed the door shut. The next morning, he was found dead by his own hand at the foot of the bed on which his dead wife lay. Dr Dick was never seen again. According to the story, he escaped via the chimney flue. The Lantern Room flue is said to have communicated with other flues and with secret passageways joining various hiding places.

Of these, three were allegedly discovered. One was by the side of a chimney over the doorway into the kitchen. Another was reached through a trapdoor in the attic. Yet another was to be found high up inside the small kitchen chimney, but, according to writer Fletcher Moss, 'no one living has ever explored it'. On stormy nights cries and muffled voices have been heard in the aforementioned chimney – echoes of the ill-fated flight. The unfortunate Dr Dick is assumed to have somehow entered it, and was asphyxiated by fumes.

Interestingly, there is indeed a secret hiding place at Plas Mawr, positioned between the Lantern Room and the Reception Room or Withdrawing Room on the first floor. It is located within the thickness of the massive chimney stack, and was probably entered from the attic.

Hodgetts suggests Robert Wynn held Catholic sympathies and 'defiantly' inscribed I.H.S over the hall fireplace. It stands for Jesus *Hominum Salvator* (Jesus, Saviour of Men). He also suggests the recusant printers from Little Orme, Llandudno (see p. 147) could have transferred their activities here.

High Street, Conwy LL32 8DE; Cadw, open part year.

7. GWYDIR CASTLE CONWY

The Wynns of Gwydir were the most powerful family in North Wales. Following the Wars of the Roses (1455–85), Maredudd ap Ieuan rebuilt a fortified hall house here from the ruins of a Glyndwr-era property owned by the Welsh knight, Hywel Coetmor. The three-storeyed Solar Tower, along with the stone-flagged and timber-floored Hall Range are attributed to this period. Maredudd's son, John (d. 1559), adopted the Wynn surname and continued with the building, reusing stone from the recently dissolved Maenan Abbey. One of his sons, Robert Wynn MP (1520–98) built Plas Mawr. Further work was carried out by John's grandson, the fire-brand antiquarian Sir John Wynn, 1st Baronet (1553–1627).

The family held Royalist sympathies. Sir John's son, Sir Richard Wynn (1588–1649), served as assistant to the Lord Chamberlain, Secretary to Prince Charles, Groom of the Bedchamber to King Charles I, and as Treasurer of the Household to Queen Henrietta Maria.

During the nineteenth century, a panelled corridor between the Hall of Meredith and the Great Hall came to be known as the Ghost Room after the sightings of a grisly spectre accompanied by the pungent odour of rotting flesh. The cause, it was said, was one of the John Wynns, who had seduced and murdered a maid and had her body walled up in a void in the chimney known as the 'priest hole'. The void exists, but whether it was ever a secret hiding place (a fire gutted large areas of the house in 1922) or, indeed, whether there is any truth to the story, is not known.

In his *Pilgrimages to Old Homes*, Fletcher Moss confused tradition with fact when he described a void under the Ghost Room's floorboards: when taken up they revealed 'unknown depths' leading to a tunnel 4.8km long! He also described a large square area of brickwork in the centre of the house that was 'never opened', behind which lies a secret staircase.

Llanrwst, Conwy LL26 0PN; variable opening part year, accommodation and events.

PRIEST
HOLES IN WALES

The Morgans of Llantarnam and the earls of Worcester were lead-ing Monmouthshire Catholics. During the mid-1590s, Robert Jones (c. 1564–1615), later the Jesuit superior, was based at Raglan Castle,[60] as a guest of Edward Somerset, 4th Earl of Somerset (c. 1550–1628). Soon after 1600, he allowed the Jesuits to establish a specially built base at Cwm in Llanrothal, north of Monmouth (just across the border in Herefordshire). The latter had many priest holes but was largely demolished in the nineteenth century.

Naturally, south-east Wales was a centre for Jesuit missionary activity. In 1907, a large mural painting recognised as 'The Adoration of the Magi', the altar piece of a secret Catholic chapel, was found in the attic of Thomas Gunter's House, Abergavenny[61] (now housed in the museum). In addition, various markings were found, including the initials 'T.G.' (Thomas Gunter), 'I.H.S' and other Jesuit symbols. Nearby, there are hides at Great Cillwch, Pitt House, Ty Mawr and Treowen.[62]

Father Philip Evans, one of the 'Forty Martyrs of England and Wales' was arrested during the Oates scare at Sker House, Porthcawl,[63] and executed in 1679. Sker House was long reputed to be riddled with secret chambers and passages, and it is likely there was at least one priest hole here. There were almost certainly priest holes at Llantarnam Abbey[64] and Cefn Mabley, Newport,[65] but these and many others were lost. No doubt others await discovery.

Holywell, 'The Lourdes of Wales', became a centre for Jesuit mission-ary activity for North Wales and Cheshire. Nearby, an unusual secret hiding place can be found in a limestone cave above Llandudno, some 25m below the top of a cliff on a steep grassy slope. In 1585, Robert Pugh, assisted by a group of priests, produced a small volume here entitled *Y Drych Cristionogawl* (*The Christian Monitor*). In 1587, a local man stumbled across the illegal printing press and alerted local Justice of the Peace, Sir Thomas Mostyn of Gloddaeth Hall. A posse was assembled but the printers escaped via a natural chimney in the cave. Hodgetts suggests they went to nearby Plas Penrhyn (Penrhyn Old Hall),[66] the sixteenth-century home of recusant Robert Pugh where there is said to be a priest hole behind a fireplace. Further east, there are secret hiding places at Plas yn y Pentre, Llangollen and Gledlom, Ysceifiog.[67]

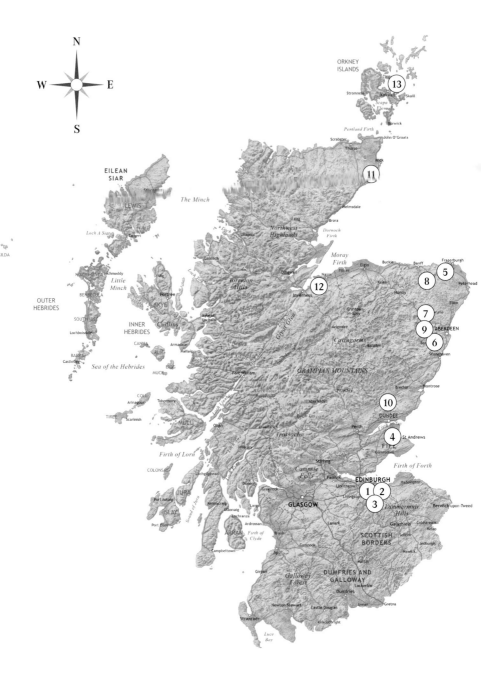

Scotland evokes images of historic cities and highland splendour, brooding towers and baronial castles. With secret chambers aplenty, the question is: where to begin?

HIDDEN BRITAIN

1. EDINBURGH CASTLE LOTHIAN

Perched on the rocky remains of a 700-million-year-old extinct volcano, Scotland's most famous castle dominates the great city. Edinburgh Castle evolved over many centuries, probably beginning when Malcolm III (1031–93) erected a wooden fortress here. St Margaret's Chapel (Edinburgh's oldest surviving building) was built by David I (c.1080–1153) as a private chapel for the royal family.

This forbidding fortress has served as a royal residence, a military citadel, a treasury, a prison and a repository for government records. It is an Aladdin's Cave of antiquities.

Among them is the 'Stone of Destiny' or 'Stone of Scone' – for centuries used in the coronation of Scottish monarchs, and later those of England and the United Kingdom. Today it is kept in the Crown Room – the same room that houses Britain's oldest Royal Regalia, the Honours of Scotland.

Two storeys of a 'lost' part of the castle were rediscovered in 1912 under the Half Moon Battery. David's Tower was an early fourteenth-century tower house commissioned by David II (1324–71). It was the location of the horrifying incident known as the *Black Dinner*.

William Crichton, Constable of Edinburgh Castle, and Sir Alexander Livingston, Constable of Stirling Castle, sought to curb the Black Douglas family's power. In 1440, Crichton invited a 16-year-old William, 6th Earl of Douglas and his younger brother to a feast at Edinburgh in the presence

Edinburgh Castle. Note the Old West Sally Port in the lower wall.

of a 10-year-old-James II (1430–60). They were brutally murdered, despite the king's pleas for their lives. Legend has it that the head of a black bull, a symbol of death, was placed on the dining table.

During World War II, David's Tower served as a hiding place for the Honours. At the Act of Union in 1707, the precious regalia had been locked away in the Crown Room of Edinburgh Castle and largely forgotten about. More than a century passed, and it was generally believed that the Scottish Crown, Sceptre and Sword of State had, at some point, been spirited away to the Tower of London.

With the support of the Prince Regent (later George IV), Sir Walter Scott organised a search. On 4 February 1818, Scott and a group of Officers of State approached the closed-up Crown Room. He described the moment of discovery to his friend, the Secretary to the Admiralty (and through him to the Prince Regent).

To J.W. Croker, esq., M.P.
The extreme solemnity of opening sealed doors of oak and iron, and finally breaking open a chest which had been shut since 7th March 1707, about a hundred and eleven years, gave a sort of interest to our researches, which I can hardly express to you, and it would be very difficult to describe the intense eagerness with which we watched the rising of the lid of the chest, and the progress of the workmen in breaking it open, which was neither an easy nor a speedy task.[68]

The regalia were found in a state of perfect preservation, wrapped in linen.

Some antiquities are less obvious. With its magnificent hammer beam roof (a faithful reproduction of the original) and a profusion of arms and armour, the early sixteenth century Great Hall in among the finest in Scotland. To the right of its massive fireplace is a spyhole or 'laird's lug', an iron-barred opening commissioned in the time of James IV (1473–1513) and allegedly used to eavesdrop on guests. Prior to Mikhail Gorbachev's visit in 1984, the KGB asked for it to be bricked up.

Although no truly secret chambers are known, there are dark dungeons and grim vaults. A deep pit prison exists beneath the floor of James VI's birth chamber, and a series of barrel-vaulted tunnels beneath the Great Hall served as a place of incarceration for prisoners of war in the late eighteenth and early nineteenth centuries.

An *unrecorded* labyrinth of tunnels is also said to exist. Legend has it that a young piper was sent in to explore them, became lost and has haunted them ever since. It is possible the legend was inspired by the extant Old West Sally Port – or, perhaps, something long forgotten.

Castle Hill, Edinburgh EH1 2NG; Historic Scotland, open all year.

2. MARY KING'S CLOSE, SOUTH BRIDGE VAULTS AND GILMERTON COVE EDINBURGH

There are secrets under Edinburgh's streets. Located on the northern side of Edinburgh's Royal Mile, beneath the site of the City Chambers, sixteenth-century Mary King's Close was abandoned in the middle of the seventeenth century and built over after outbreaks of the plague. How it came to be called Mary King's Close is a matter of speculation, but the eerie subterranean streetscape is today a tourist attraction.

Completed in 1788, the famous Edinburgh Vaults or South Bridge Vaults are a complex series of chambers formed in the nineteen viaduct arches of the South Bridge between the Old Town and Southside. Though used initially for storage and trade, the vaults were flood prone and gradually abandoned. However, as the Industrial Revolution progressed they became a hellish slum and a notorious red light district. Crimes, including robbery and murder, plagued the vaults and Burke and Hare, the infamous serial killers who sold corpses to medical schools, are said to have hunted for victims there.

Located in the old mining village of Gilmerton on the city's southern fringes, Gilmerton Cove is an elaborate series of rock-cut passages of uncertain origin. Theories about their use range from cultish drinking den to secret Covenanter's refuge.

According to tradition, the passages link up with a wider network of tunnels, one of which leads to Drum House.

Mary King's Close: The Real Mary King's Close, 2 Warriston's Close, High Street, Edinburgh EH1 1PG. Open all year.

South Bridge Vaults: 28 South Bridge, Edinburgh EH1 1LL. Mercat Tours offer history and ghost walks.

Gilmerton Cove: 16 Drum Street, Edinburgh EH17 8QH. Tours by appointment.

3. LAURISTON CASTLE EDINBURGH

Set in parkland overlooking the Firth of Forth, this quirky mansion contains hidden stairs, a secret chamber and a cleverly concealed door.

Built in around 1590 for master of the Scottish mint and 7th Laird of Merchiston Sir Archibald Napier (1534–1608), the existing T-plan tower house replaced a castle that was burned by the English in 1544. By far its most famous resident was the rakish financier, duellist and gambler John Law (1671–1729).

In 1827, Thomas Allan, a banker and mineralogist, commissioned William Burn (1789–1870) to extend Lauriston in the Jacobean style. Then, in 1902, it was acquired by prosperous local cabinetmaker William Robert Reid, and he and his wife Margaret filled the house with a collection of fine furniture and antiques. The Reids had no heirs and left their home to the Scottish nation on the condition that it should be preserved unchanged.

On the east side of the Oak Room in the old tower an innocent-looking window shutter swings out to reveal a spiral staircase up to the Napier's secret room. Measuring 1.5m sq., the 'prophet's chamber' or 'laird's lug' is located in the wall thickness between the first and second floors. Before a new ceiling was fitted in the nineteenth century it contained what is thought to have been a covert listening aperture or spyhole to the room below (by tradition, the hall).

Meanwhile, the well-stocked nineteenth-century library has a hinged Edwardian bookcase. It doubles as a 'secret' door – an escape route, via more hidden stairs, to the tranquil gardens.

Edinburgh EH4 5QD; museum; guided tour only, limited opening all year.

4. ST ANDREWS CASTLE FIFE

This fascinating castle stands on a rugged sea promontory and served as a bishop's palace, and as a prison. St Andrews was a key site during the Scottish Wars of Independence and the Reformation, and its ruins are a reminder of a turbulent, bloody past.

First erected in the late twelfth century, the castle was substantially rebuilt towards the end of the fourteenth century when a pentagon-shaped curtain wall was thrown up around the enclosure, two towers were erected and the old Fore Tower was rebuilt.

The sixteenth century saw a further phase of rebuilding following a siege of 1546–47. At a time of religious tension during the sixteenth century, the last pre-Reformation Scottish Cardinal, David Beaton (c.1494–1546) unilaterally ordered the burning at the stake of the itinerant Protestant preacher George

Wishart (c. 1513–46), allegedly in front of the castle (while Cardinal Beaton and his entourage watched the grizzly spectacle from an upper window).

Then, at daybreak on 29 May 1546, Protestant reformers Norman Leslie and William Kirkcaldy gained entry to the castle, killing a porter in the process. They murdered Cardinal Beaton, mutilated his corpse and hung it from a window.

Protestants held the castle for a year against Catholic forces led by Mary of Guise (mother of Mary, Queen of Scots). During the siege the attackers sank a mine, tunnelling through solid rock with the aim of reaching the Fore Tower. The defenders discovered the plan and sank a counter mine to meet the attacker and fight them off.

Rediscovered in 1879, both tunnels are around 2.1m high and 1.8m wide. Today, visitors are invited to explore these rare vestiges of medieval siege warfare.

Further evidence of dangerous times can be found below the north-west tower. Cut in solid rock, the castle's bottle dungeon was one of the most infamous prisons in Scotland. Measuring 2m in diameter at the top, 4.8m at the bottom and some 7m deep, few left it alive.

St Andrews KY16 9AR; Historic Scotland, open all year except Christmas Day and Boxing Day.

5. The Wine Tower Aberdeenshire

◇◇

Aberdeenshire was a bastion of the old faith and a number of its buildings contain Roman Catholic symbols from the post-Reformation period. In addition, some were equipped with secret chambers.

Dramatically sited on an exposed headland, the curiously named Wine Tower was built in the sixteenth century by the Frasers of Philorth. Its purpose is unclear. The extant structure contains three storeys, all vaulted. The tower is reached via a difficult path and metres from the front door rocks fall precipitously down to the sea at high water. Immediately below is a cave called Selches Hole, now inaccessible. Dark and eerie, the basement is lit by a useless gun port, just 15cm wide, carried diagonally through the massive wall and arranged in such a way that it was impossible to see what was going on inside.

The tower lacks internal stairs and there is no way between the basement and the first floor. Lit by an insignificant sea-facing window, the first floor was reached via a trapdoor above and the entry to the second floor – a secret chapel – was via an external ladder. It contains a fireplace and an impressive series of carved heraldic pendant bosses. At its north end is an Arma Christi, Christ's armorial coat of arms.

Legend has it that Alexander Fraser, 8th Laird of Philorth (c. 1536–1623) locked his daughter Isobel in the second-floor chamber after she fell in love with a lowly piper. The piper, meanwhile, was chained up in the cave below.

SCOTTISH
TOWER HOUSES

The evolution of castles in Scotland followed much the same pattern as that of England and Wales. From the fourteenth century, however, the Scots in particular chose to build vertically. Why? Compact but formidable, tower houses hail from a time when a man's home needed quite literally to be his castle. They provided local lairds with the comforts and status of a medieval house – hall, solar, chapel and so on – but up-ended for protection. They were often built with walls many feet thick to an L- or Z-plan with a 'jam' or wing containing accommodation or stairs in the flanking towers, and were surrounded by banks or ditches.

Tower houses are well known for unusual architectural features. Often, there were pit prisons and small secret chambers in the thickness of walls. Some were equipped with spyholes; others had 'lugs' (channels thought to have enabled the eavesdropper to hear what was going on in different rooms). For examples, see Castle Fraser on pp. 157–61.

Staircases were ingeniously constructed in the wall thickness to deter intruders. They did not always go up the same corner, forcing an intruder to cross the floor (e.g. Affleck Castle, Angus[69]). Flights crossed over other flights, had no exit to floors or were accessed via concealed stairs.

There were false storeys and unexpected changes of floor levels to baffle and disorientate. The now ruinous Elphinstone Tower, East Lothian, had a honeycomb of chambers, passages and stairways built into its walls that would surely have presented an intruder with a problem. It also had a set of secret rooms in the north-west corner of the tower, a chamber off the flue of the Great Hall fireplace and a spyhole.

The sixteenth and nineteenth centuries saw new structures built in the Scottish baronial style of architecture around earlier structures, which is why so many of Scotland's grand 'castles' have, at their core, a mysterious old tower house.

He drowned during a storm tide and, upon hearing this news, Isobel flung herself from the tower.

Aberdeenshire AB43 9DU; adjacent to Kinnaird Castle (now the Museum of Scottish Lighthouses), access and tours by arrangement.

6. DRUM CASTLE ABERDEENSHIRE

<><><><><><><><><><><><><><><><><><><><><><><><><><><><><><><><><><><><><><>

It was William de Irwin of Bonshaw (*c.*1260–1333) who won the seat of the Chief of the Clan Irvine. The family crest, which features holly leaves and the motto *'Sub sole sub umbra virens'* ('Flourishing under Sun and Cloud') was traditionally bestowed upon the clan after William sheltered Robert the Bruce from the forces of Edward I under a holly tree. In reality, it was for years of loyalty to 'The Bruce', including services rendered at the Battle of Bannockburn (1314). For twenty-four generations, Drum remained in Irvine hands, until 1976 when it was taken over by the National Trust for Scotland.

As Catholic Royalists in hostile territory, Drum's Clan Irvine owners certainly *needed* a secret chamber. When the Covenanting (equivalent of Roundhead) Rebellion began in 1639 between Charles I and the Scottish Presbyterians, the castle was attacked and plundered repeatedly. Alexander, the 10th Laird (*c.* 1594–1657), was an ardent Royalist in a district of Covenanters, as were his two eldest sons, Alexander and Robert. Both were captured. Robert died in the dungeons of Edinburgh Castle, but Alexander was released after the Royalist victory at the Battle of Kilsyth in 1645. He went on to become the 11th Laird.

Another Alexander Irvine, the 17th Laird (d. 1761), was a Jacobite who fought for Charles Edward Stuart (Bonnie Prince Charlie). He escaped after the Battle of Culloden in 1746 and sheltered in Drum's secret room. When pursuing Redcoats (British soldiers) arrived, his sister, Mary Irvine, misdirected them. The soldiers did, however, make off with more Irvine family wealth, having spotted where it was buried in newly dug earth.

Set amidst the Royal Forest of Drum and comprising the usual arrangement of high, thick-walled medieval tower house, three-storey Jacobean mansion and Victorian extension, Drum today is one of the most beautiful castles in Royal Deeside.

Investigators recently uncovered two hidden chambers in the medieval tower, blocked off in the 1840s when a new library was built in the Great Hall (obscuring window openings that were visible from the outside). The original doorway entrance to the Great Hall was found in the innermost chamber, along with a medieval garderobe (privy). In addition, a second chamber came to light, thought to be the 17th Laird's secret hiding place.

Drumoak AB31 5EY; National Trust for Scotland, open part year.

7. FETTERNEAR HOUSE ABERDEENSHIRE

After the Scottish Reformation, Fetternear became the principal seat of the recusant Leslies of Balquhain. Obscured by a nineteenth-century neo-Gothic façade, the oldest part of the house consisted of a tower house built about 1566. To this Count Patrick Leslie, 15th Baron, added the central part of the house in around 1691–93. His coat of arms is still displayed over the main entrance, defiantly incorporating Leslie's coronet of a Count of the Holy Roman Empire, above which is a stone bearing the rare twin religious monograms I.H.S and M.R.A, which stand for Jesus *Hominum Salvator* (Jesus, Saviour of Men) and Maria *Regina Angelorum* (Mary, Queen of Angels). I H S was, of course, associated with the Society of Jesus, and Count Patrick's brother had been Rector of the Scots' College in Rome (founded in 1600 by Pope Clement VIII).

Fetternear was besieged twice by Covenanters in the 1640s, and, in an anonymous pamphlet published in 1714, George Leslie was accused of being 'a Popish Gentleman' whose family harboured Jesuits.

It is said the old house had many a priest hole, including one that was located in a wall behind a moveable bookcase. In Bonnie Prince Charlie's time, a troop of Redcoats arrived at the door. The male inhabitants hid in priest holes while the lady of the house went to the door and protested against the soldiers entering. 'It were a shame,' she said, 'to enter by force a house where there were but a few lone women.' The confidence she displayed deceived the officer in charge, and the Redcoats left.

Fetternear fell into disrepair following a fire in 1919. The forlorn remains stand next to another site of archaeological importance: the summer residence of the bishops of Aberdeen, otherwise known as the Bishop's Palace.

Kemnay, Inverurie AB51 5LY; private, visible from metalled paths.

8. FYVIE CASTLE ABERDEENSHIRE

This grand, five-towered baronial fortress reflects many periods and incorporates ancient fabric (perhaps as early as the thirteenth century). The castle's atmospheric interior contains opulent, Edwardian-era furniture and walls richly adorned with fine paintings, tapestries, arms and armour.

Like Glamis (see *Introduction*), Fyvie is reputed to have a secret vault under its charter room (located on the first floor of the Meldrum Tower). This one is said to contain untold riches – but a death curse awaits anyone who breaks into it!

Turriff, AB53 8JS; National Trust for Scotland, open part year.

9. CASTLE FRASER ABERDEENSHIRE

Amidst a sublime, eighteenth-century landscape stands one of the finest baronial tower houses anywhere in Scotland.

Originally named Muchall-in-Mar, Michael Fraser, the 6th Laird of Fraser began converting a pre-existing, rectangular tower house into an elaborate, Z-plan castle in around 1575. It was finished by his son, Andrew Fraser, the 7th Laird (created Lord Fraser 1633). It was he who installed a curious and disputed architectural feature known as the Laird's Lug.

The chamber was discovered in the early nineteenth century. A friend of Sir Walter Scott, the artist and antiquarian James Skene (1775–1864) described it in the first of two unpublished manuscripts kept at Edinburgh City Library, entitled, *Domestic and Ecclesiastical Architecture of Scotland*.

In the Worked Room above the hall (traditionally the laird's bedroom), there are several closets in the thickness of the wall, and the entrance to one of them is concealed by a window shutter. When Skene visited, the entire floor was covered with rough stone, which he thought would have been covered with peat or wood for the fire, further concealing irregularities in the stonework. When the household switched to coal, a maid was cleaning the closet when the floor gave way, and hearing a dislodged stone fall into a veritable abyss, she beat a hasty retreat. For a while, she kept the discovery a secret and avoided being sent to the 'picture room of the auld kings' (so named after old pictures of the Stuart kings that used to hang in the apartment). However, the void was discovered soon afterwards.

The 30cm by 38cm hole looked like a chimney vent through the floor, into which a stone similar to the rest was fitted. A lantern was lowered into it and a boy sent down 'with no small reluctance on his part'. Next, a long ladder was produced so Skene could squeeze through the narrow shaft into the chamber. He found what at first appeared to be a typical place of concealment – a 2m by 1m, 2m-high vaulted chamber with loop holes. There was also a conduit to the hall below, and when he tested a theory, Skene 'distinctly heard what was spoken' in an arched window recess with a stone seat all around – a place where conversations might well take place. He called the contrivance an 'ear' or 'lug'.

Inspired by the Laird's Lug, Sir Walter Scott wove eavesdropping devices into his stories, in each case linking them to the name of Dionysius after a Sicilian cave known as the Ear of Dionysius. In fact, Scott used lugs as plot devices in no less than three of his novels: *A Legend of Montrose* (1819), *Fortunes of Nigel* (1822) and *Count Robert, of Paris* (1832):

> 'Stone walls can hear' – said the Follower, lowering his voice. 'Dionysius the Tyrant, I have read, had an Ear which conveyed to him the secrets spoken within the state-prison at Syracuse'.

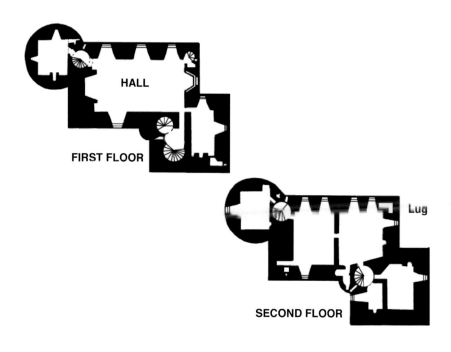

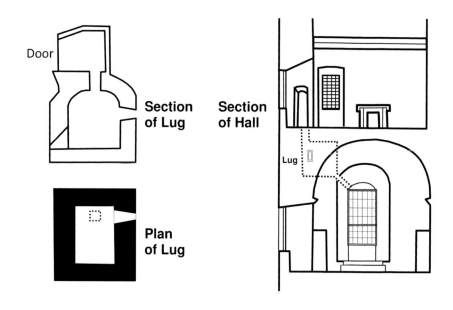

Details of the Laird's Lug at Castle Fraser (after MacGibbon and Ross, 1887)

Skene and Scott were convinced the Laird's Lug was a room built for espionage, but others have demurred, suggesting it would be too small and uncomfortable, or that it was merely a store room, or even a small dungeon. We can probably discount the latter. It would have been absurdly difficult to manhandle a prisoner into the chamber, it is accessed from a high-status bedroom and it is difficult to understand why a conduit would be required.

Actually, there is sufficient evidence to conclude that it was a secret hiding place. For one, there is a reason for it to be there. The Frasers were Protestant but, as we have seen, seventeenth-century Scotland was a dangerous place (whatever one's religious denomination). That, after all, is why tower houses were built. A security-conscious laird might well commission a secret hiding place cum strong room for his family, muniments (documents) and valuables. A method for covert communication might enhance its effectiveness – 'it's safe to come out, m' lord'. Alternatively, the conduit could simply be a vent (note the similarities between the Laird's Lug and the secret chamber at Castle Sinclair Girnigoe). Whatever the conduit's purpose, the Laird's Lug exhibits strong evidence of concealment, both in terms of the location of the chamber in the thickness of the wall and the stone entrance cover (since replaced with a modern trapdoor). The fact that the feature was for many years 'lost' is a testament to how effective the concealment was.

But was it too small? No. Most secret hiding places are of a similar size. They had to be small to remain secret! If this were England, the Laird's Lug would pass for one of Nicholas Owen's hides (often created in the thickness of walls), and if we recall Hodgetts' 'average' priest hole, which was 'an almost featureless space, perhaps 8ft by 3ft and 5ft high, only identifiable by its flooring and by its entrance ... most often a trap-door in a garderobe closet or other dark corner', the similarities are striking.

Lugs were created elsewhere. The similarity of the arrangement at Castle Sinclair Girnigoe has already been noted, and there is a Laird's Lug-like secret chamber in the end wall of the solar at Tolquhon Castle, Aberdeenshire[70] (reached by a hatch from the floor above), and something similar at Castle Menzies, Perthshire.[71] Further examples can be found at Muchalls Castle, Aberdeenshire[72] (between the Great Hall fireplace and the mural chamber off the laird's bedroom), Affleck Castle, Angus (between a latrine in the upper part of the 'jam' on the second floor and the Lord's Hall), Lauriston Castle (p. 152) and at the now-ruinous Elphinstone Tower, East Lothian. Prior to Mikhail Gorbachev's 1984 visit to Edinburgh Castle, the KGB insisted that a laird's lug in the Great Hall was blocked up (p. 149)

That they appear to have been fairly common suggests a practical primary purpose. Of the various possibilities, the most likely explanation is that the majority were air conduits (vents). Vents would provide an occupant with fresh air, but more importantly, they would help keep documents dry and at a constant temperature. Of course, they would also act as sound conduits – but whether this was a conscious feature of their design is a matter for speculation.

CHAMBERS
OF SECRETS

Now a celebrated public school, Gordonstoun began as a sixteenth-century tower house. Originally named 'Plewlands', it was put up in a remote, midge-ridden bog (the estate was known as 'Bog o' Plewlands). Despite insalubrious beginnings, the estate prospered. Plewlands was remodelled by the Scottish Roman Catholic conspirator George Gordon, 1st Marquis of Huntly (1562–1636).

Though well hidden, the old tower house forms the core of the present mansion. However, it is Huntly's additions that excite most interest – for he created complex hides between the vaults and the first floor, along with a well inside the walls for withstanding a siege. 'In the vault above the dungeon area in the west wing was a warren of secret stairs and passages,' wrote former Warden Henry Brereton. 'To this day, two concealed trap-doors give access to small secret chambers deliberately incorporated into the original house by the First Marquis of Huntly.'

Equally colourful was Sir Robert Gordon, the so-called Wizard of Gordonstoun. Born in 1647, he became laird in 1688. Tradition has it that whilst studying at the University of Padua, Italy, he became interested in alchemy, and to further his knowledge made a pact with the Devil. It was believed he cast no shadow, and none of the people around would venture near the house after nightfall. Sir Robert built an amphitheatre-like ring of estate buildings, paradoxically called the Round Square. Naturally, it was believed to have been designed to magical proportions: a circle of protection to stop the Devil claiming his soul.

The intrigue continues. Putrid smells close to the small kitchen recently led to the discovery of a waterlogged dungeon in the west wing, boarded up over a century ago and forgotten about. Over 4m deep, the only light would have been provided by a candle placed on a crude shelf in the stone wall.

It begs the question: what else awaits discovery?

Sadly, the lower portion of the Laird's Lug at Castle Fraser was destroyed in the nineteenth century when a pipe organ was installed in the Great Hall (since removed). As a consequence, its acoustic qualities can no longer be tested.

Sauchen, Inverurie AB51 7LD; National Trust for Scotland, open part year.

10. GLAMIS CASTLE ANGUS

The towering seat of the earls of Strathmore (and childhood home of the late Queen Mother) is associated with a famous and hotly disputed secret chamber story. See *Introduction*.

Glamis DD8 1RJ; private castle, open part year.

Glamis Castle.

◇◇

The dramatic ruins of Castle Sinclair Girnigoe are located on a spectacular, wave-battered peninsula overlooking Sinclair Bay. Now recognised as being of national and international significance, this complex, sprawling castle began in the late fifteenth century when William Sinclair, 2nd Earl of Caithness (1459–1513) built a five-storey, L-plan tower house, probably upon an earlier fortification. In 1606, new structures were added, including a gatehouse and other buildings, surrounded by a curtain wall and connected to the rest of the castle by a drawbridge over a rock-cut ravine. At this time the castle's name was changed from Girnigoe to Sinclair – but the old name persisted.

Surviving architectural features include intriguing passages, vaulted rooms and a small but sophisticated secret chamber, located under the first floor of the tower house and not visible from outside. Accessed through a trap in the solar (the only way in), it is above the kitchen. The chamber has a vaulted ceiling, a vent communicating with the kitchen flue and concealed loops that could be closed against the weather. It is thought to have been used as a secret muniment room (a hiding place for valuables, especially documents), but if the need arose, it was certainly capable of concealing a person.

Given its size and location amidst high-status residential quarters, the chamber is unlikely to have been used as a prison. Much has been said about a dark dungeon in which George Sinclair, 4th Earl of Caithness (1527–82) famously imprisoned his son John, for illegally extorting goods or some other misdemeanour – but its location (assuming it existed) is uncertain.

John died from dehydration after being given a final meal of salted beef – or so the story goes. Actually, he escaped in 1575 with the help of two brothers, and almost certainly did not die in the castle.

The 4th Earl was succeeded by his grandson, the 'wicked' 5th Earl, George III (1582–1643). Lawless and debt-ridden, he ran an illegal mint. According to tradition, it was located below the castle in a recess called 'the Cote'. Naturally, a romantic rumour sprang up about it being connected to the Earl's bedchamber via a hatch and secret passage. That, of course, is unlikely.

It seems that two interesting (but unconnected) features have been used to embellish the story: the tower house secret chamber and a surviving sally port.

At the eastern end of the peninsula, within the East Barbican enclosure, there is a trap stair. It provides access, by means of a rock-cut stair, to a landing area. A further flight of stairs then leads to an arched opening through the rock face, and on to the sea shore.

5km north of Wick, Caithness; Clan Sinclair Trust, visible from access road, open part year.

12. Cawdor Castle Highland

By Sinel's death, I know, I am Thane of Glamis:
But how of Cawdor? The Thane of Cawdor lives
A prosperous gentleman; and, to be king
Stands not within the prospect of belief

Cawdor Castle and the thanes of Cawdor will forever be associated with
Macbeth – but this did not please the 5th Earl Cawdor. Fed up with the endless questions, he said, 'I wish the Bard had never written his dammed play!'

His reasons were clear. The historical Macbeth ruled Scotland from 1040–57,
after his forces defeated and killed Duncan I (r. 1034–40) at Pitgaveny, near
Elgin (in the play, Macbeth kills him in his sleep). However, the 1st Thane
(broadly equivalent to a baron) did not appear on the scene until the end of the
thirteenth century! Although not explicitly mentioned in *Macbeth*, the earliest
documented date for the castle is 1454, when a building licence was granted
to William Calder (original spelling), 6th Thane of Cawdor. What we see today
is a courtyard castle of various dates: a largely fifteenth-century, five-storey
crenellated tower house that was probably begun in the late fourteenth century, sixteenth-century north and west wings and numerous later additions.
Clearly, the castle did not exist in the mid-eleventh century.

That is not to say it lacks romance. Curiously, the tower was built around a
living holly tree (long thought to be a hawthorn), the remains of which are on

Cawdor Castle.

display in situ at the base of the tower. For some, this amazing sight will bring to mind the White Tree of Gondor, from J.R.R. Tolkien's *The Lord of the Rings*, and it is tempting to believe the similarity is more than mere coincidence.

According to legend, the Thane of Cawdor had a small castle nearby but wanted something grander. After having a dream about how to decide where to build his new tower he set to it, according to those instructions. He attached a load of gold to a donkey and set it free. His tower would be built wherever the animal chose to rest. The donkey lay down next to a tree, and it is around this that Cawdor was built. Interestingly, radiocarbon dating of the wood has dated the tree to approximately 1372, so it is near enough contemporary with the early tower.

Cawdor today is certainly atmospheric, helped by the fact that it largely escaped the changes that were so fashionable in the eighteenth century as the thanes decamped to their estates in Wales during the first Jacobite rising, leaving a factor in charge. They returned in the nineteenth century. Patrick Fraser Tytler (1791–1849) wrote a description that appeared in the second volume of *Edinburgh Philosophical Transactions*:

> The whole of Cawdor Castle is peculiarly calculated to impress the mind with a retrospect of past ages, feudal customs, and deeds of darkness. Its iron-grated doors, its ancient tapestry, hanging loosely over secret doors and hidden passages, its winding staircases, its rattling drawbridge, all conspire to excite the most gloomy imagery in the mind.

Fraser Tytler mentioned a 'secret apartment', said to have concealed Lord Lovat, 'Never was anything so artfully contrived', he says:

> It is placed immediately beneath the rafters of the roof. By means of a ladder you are conducted by the side of one part of a sloping roof into a kind of channel between two, such as frequently serves to convey rainwater into pipes for a reservoir. Proceeding along this channel, you arrive at the foot of a stone staircase, which leads up one side of the roof to the right, and is so artfully contrived as to appear a part of the ornaments of the building when beheld at a distance. At the end of this staircase is a room with a single window near the floor.

In his *Room Notes*, the 6th Earl Cawdor gives a less florid description:

> In the gable above the front door can be seen the small lancet window of a concealed room where the 11th Lord Lovat is said to have hidden for three days in 1699 ... Above this same gable, to your left, is a corbelled projection which was a murder hole.

Meanwhile, there is something sinister in the Thorn Tree Room at the base of the tower. A trapdoor conceals a chute in the thickness of the wall, down which an unfortunate victim might be thrown into the secret bottle dungeon. There is no way out!

Cawdor, Nairn IV12 5RD; private castle, open part year.

13. BALFOUR CASTLE ORKNEY ISLANDS

◇◇◇

This nineteenth-century, baronial-style mansion was designed by the eminent Edinburgh architect David Bryce for Colonel David Balfour, 4th Laird of Balfour.

Set amidst Orkney's largest wooded area but within close sight of the sea, the present house incorporates a late eighteenth-century house called Cliffdale, built by David's grandfather, Thomas Balfour, after he purchased the estate of Sound.

Accompanied by his wife Eleanor, David toured Italy acquiring ideas and works of art whilst the new castle was being built. As a consequence, it contains many beautiful rooms, and the interior owes much to a team of thirty Italian craftsmen who were employed during its construction. There is also a fine collection of pictures, trophies and curiosities. Chief among the latter is the contrivance in the atmospheric library to the rear of the building.

Balfour Castle.

A false sets of bookshelves here leads to a secret passage to the drawing room near the conservatory door. It was a useful addition, allowing members of the Balfour family to mysteriously 'disappear' whenever an unwanted visitor arrived ...

Cluedo, anyone?

Shapinsay, Orkney KW17 2DY; hotel, conference and events venue.

Balfour Castle interior.

Balfour Castle's secret gib door.

5

GLOSSARY & KEY HISTORICAL EVENTS

Abbey: A group of buildings housing a Catholic or, more recently, an Anglican monastery or convent, whose head is an Abbot or Abbess.

Anglican: A branch of the church that began in England, where it is referred to as the Church of England.

Ashlar: Masonry blocks with even faces and square edges, used for the facing of walls.

Attic: The space below the pitched roof of a building.

Babington Plot: Plot of 1586 to assassinate the Protestant Elizabeth I and replace her with her Roman Catholic cousin, Mary, Queen of Scots. Named after Catholic conspirator Anthony Babington (1561–86), its discovery led to Mary's trial and execution in 1587.

Barrel vault: A semi-cylindrical vault.

Basement: Lower storey of a building beneath the principal one.

Battlement: A parapet with a series of rectangular indentations or raised portions. The gaps are termed 'crenels', and adding crenels to a previously unbroken parapet is termed crenellation.

Buttress: A vertical member of stone or brick, built against a wall to strengthen or support it.

Catholic: Of the ancient Roman Catholic faith; an adherent of Catholicism.

Cellar: A room or space, usually beneath the ground or under a building. For centuries cellars have been used for storage, the sale of goods and other purposes. Many were associated with the wine trade (there are fine examples at Winchelsea, Southampton and Norwich) and the word 'cellar' and 'tavern' were sometimes interchangeable during the medieval period.

Corbel: A bracket or weight carrying member.

Counter-Reformation: Essentially the response of the Roman Catholic Church to the Protestant Reformation, beginning with the Council of Trent (1545–63), held in Trento and Bologna, Italy.

Covenanter: A Scottish Presbyterian who supported the National Covenant of 1638 or the Solemn League and Covenant of 1643. The movement's purpose was to unite the Scottish nation against the Stuart King's efforts to impose an episcopal church and government with the King as its spiritual head. Covenanters allied themselves with the English Parliament during the Wars of the Three Kingdoms (1639–51).

Crenellation: See Battlement.

Crypt: An underground room, often a burial chamber below the east end of a church.

Dissolution of the Monasteries: The first Act of Supremacy (1534) extinguished all papal authority and made Henry VIII the Supreme Head of the Church in England and Wales. Between 1536 and 1541 monasteries, priories, convents and friaries in England, Wales and Ireland were disbanded, their income appropriated and their assets disposed of.

Eaves: Overhanging edge of a pitched roof.

Elizabethan style: An architectural style of the reign of Elizabeth I (r. 1558–1603). Combining Tudor and European Renaissance elements, the Elizabethan style is characterised by tall square houses with symmetrical towers and large mullioned windows, long galleries, intricate strapwork (a form of decorative surround) and tall, decorated chimneys. High-status houses of this period were often built to an E-plan, in honour of the queen.

English Civil War: A series of armed conflicts between 1642 and 1651, largely a consequence of King Charles I's efforts to impose taxation without Parliament's consent and changes to the form of Anglican worship. On one side were the Parliamentarians ('Roundheads'), on the other were Royalists ('Cavaliers'). It resulted in the trial and execution of Charles I and the exile of his son, Charles II, after the Parliamentarian victory at the Battle of Worcester on 3 September 1661. At first, the monarchy was replaced with the Commonwealth of England (1649–53), during which time England (which at that time included Wales), and later Scotland and Ireland, was ruled as a republic. From 1653 to 1659 Oliver Cromwell, and then briefly his son Richard, reigned as Lord Protector, closely emulating the deposed monarchy.

Gable: Triangular part of the wall at the end of a pitched roof.

Garderobe: A small chamber containing a latrine.

Garret: A habitable attic room.

Glorious Revolution: The deposition in 1688 of the Catholic James II (James VII of Scotland) by a union of Parliamentarians, followed by the accession of his Protestant daughter, Mary, and her Dutch-Protestant husband, William III of Orange-Nassau (William of Orange).

Gunpowder Plot: Also known as the Jesuit Treason. On Sunday 20 May 1604 five fanatical Roman Catholics led by Robert Catesby met at the Duck and Drake inn just off the Strand, London. Their leader's plan was simple: blow up King James I, along with his Parliament, instigate a revolt and install James'

9-year-old daughter Elizabeth as the Catholic head of state. Among the group of was a York-born mercenary named Guy Fawkes.

Catesby and two fellow conspirators were already under surveillance and the haphazard recruitment of eight additional plotters further compromised secrecy. One of them sent an anonymous warning letter to Lord Monteagle, a Roman Catholic peer:

> 26 October 1605
> My lord, out of the love I bear to some of your friends, I have a care of your preservation, therefore I would advise you as you tender your life to devise some excuse to shift your attendance at this parliament, for God and man have concurred to punish the wickedness of this time, and think not slightly of this advertisement, but retire yourself into your country, where you may expect the event in safety, for though there be no appearance of any stir, yet I say they shall receive a terrible blow this parliament and yet they shall not see who hurts them, this counsel is not to be condemned because it may do you good and can do you no harm, for the danger is past as soon as you have burnt the letter and I hope God will give you the grace to make good use of it, to whose holy protection I commend you.

Uncertain about its meaning, Monteagle showed the letter to Secretary of State Robert Cecil.

Early on the morning of 5 November 1605, Guy Fawkes was apprehended in a vault below the House of Lords with thirty-six barrels of gunpowder. Subsequently, he was tortured, hanged, drawn and quartered. The rest of the plotters fled to the country but were either killed whilst resisting arrest or captured.

Lord Monteagle was married to Elizabeth Tresham, the sister of the reckless and unstable Francis Tresham of Rushton Hall, Northamptonshire (the last to be admitted to the group). Although he vehemently denied it, most historians suspect he was the letter's author.

Hair plaster: A type of lime plaster that incorporated animal hair (typically cattle) as a fibrous binder.

Hall house: A type of vernacular house with a high-roofed hall as the principal apartment.

Interregnum: A period when England had no king, from the execution of Charles I in 1649 to the Restoration under Charles II in 1660. England was a Commonwealth from 1649 to 1653 and was organised as a Protectorate from 1653 to 1659.

Jacobean style: A style of architecture of the reign James I and VI (r. 1603-25). The Jacobean style is similar to the Elizabethan style but richer, and more extravagant with Flemish, French and Italian Renaissance influences.

Jacobite: A supporter of the exiled House of Stuart after the deposition of James II (Latin: *Jacobus*) during the Glorious Revolution of 1688.

Jacobite Risings: A movement between 1688 and 1746 that sought the restoration of the Roman Catholic Stuart King, James II (James VII of Scotland) and his descendants following the Glorious Revolution of 1688. The most serious risings occurred 1715–16 and 1745–46, and are known respectively as the First Jacobite Rebellion ('The Fifteen') and the Second Jacobite Rebellion ('The Forty-Five').

Jesuit: A member of the Society of Jesus, a male Roman Catholic religious order founded by a Spanish noble, Saint Ignatius Loyola (1491–1556). Jesuits became an important component of the Counter-Reformation and efforts to stem the tide of Protestantism.

Joist: Horizontal member supporting a floor or ceiling.

Justice of the Peace: An official responsible for the administration and maintenance of civil discipline.

Lath and plaster: Used to create interior partition walls and ceilings. Consists of narrow strips of wood (laths) nailed to vertical wooden battens, upon which plaster is applied. Good soundproofing qualities.

Loophole: A vertical slit in the wall of a building.

Machicolation: Opening between the supporting corbels (brackets or weight-carrying members) of a projecting parapet. They allowed objects to be dropped on attackers.

Manor: An area of land under the control of a feudal lord.

Manor house: The principal residence within a manor.

Mass: Celebration of the Eucharist – presided over by a priest and in which the congregation takes part.

Mullion: Vertical member dividing the lights of a window.

Muniments room: A room for important legal records such as title deeds or charters, often a specially constructed strong room.

Mural passage / chamber: A passage or room in the thickness of a wall.

Newel stair: A stair that ascends around a central supporting newel (pillar). Called a spiral stair when the shaft is circular, a winder when the compartment is rectangular.

Panelling (or wainscoting): Wide, thin sheets of wood (panels), almost always oak, framed together by thicker strips of wood and used to decorate walls, ceilings, doors and furniture. Often richly carved, wood panelling is especially characteristic of Tudor, Elizabethan and Jacobean architectural styles.

Papist: A person associated with the Roman Catholic Church.

Parapet: A low defensive wall.

Penal times: A period between the sixteenth and eighteenth centuries during which various anti-Catholic (penal) laws were introduced.

Postern gate: A secondary gateway or back door.

Priest hole: A concealed hiding place in the house of a Roman Catholic. The majority were built during the reigns of Elizabeth I (r. 1558–1603) and James I (r. 1603–25). The diminutive Jesuit lay brother Nicholas Owen ('Little John') was the greatest exponent of the craft. Owen died under torture in the Tower of London in 1606.

Concealed in a wide variety of ways, they generally fall into the following categories:

Conversions: e.g. of garderobe closets and drains.

Exploitation [of redundant space]: e.g. under stairs.

Excavation: e.g. in the thickness of walls.

Additions: e.g. the creation of new walls, partitions and ceilings.

Priory: A monastic house whose head is a prior or prioress.

Protestant Reformation: The schism within Western Christianity precipitated and largely defined by the German Augustinian monk Martin Luther (1483–1586), John Calvin (1509–64) and other early Protestants.

Protestantism: A Christian religious movement that began in 1517 when German Augustinian monk Martin Luther (1483–1546) published *The Ninety-Five Theses on the Power and Efficacy of Indulgences*. It attacked the corruptions of the Catholic Church – in particular the practice of selling indulgences, and questioned the doctrine of the merits of saints. A Protestant is an adherent of Protestantism.

Pursuivant: A mercenary-like state official with the power to execute warrants for search and arrest, used particularly for hunting Roman Catholic priests and those who harboured them.

Recusant: The term (from the Latin *recusare* – to refuse) was a label assigned to those who remained loyal to the Roman Catholic Church and did not attend compulsory Church of England services.

Restoration: The event in 1660 by which the English, Scottish and Irish monarchies were restored under Charles II.

Sacristy: A room attached to a church, in which the sacred vessels, vestments and other items connected with the religious services of the building are kept.

Sally port: A postern (secondary gate) or a subterranean passage from the inner works to the outer works of a fortification, intended as a passage for the garrison to *sally* from, or pass through. Examples at Windsor (page p. 28) Warwick (page p. 61) and Edinburgh (page p. 89)

Screen: A partition or enclosure separating a portion of a room or church from the rest.

Screens passage: A screened-off entrance passage between a great hall and the service rooms, often supporting a minstrel's gallery.

Secret chamber: A concealed area, space or room.

Secret chapel: Clandestine place of worship, often a long, low room in the upper part of a Catholic's house. The building of Catholic chapels was legalised by the Roman Catholic Relief Act 1791.

Secret passageway/tunnel: A concealed route used for stealthy travel.

Society of Jesus: See Jesuit.

Solar: The upper living room of a medieval house.

Timber framing: A method of construction by which walls are built of timber framework and the spaces filled in by plaster or brickwork.

Transom: Horizontal member dividing the lights of a window.

Truss: Triangular frame bearing a roof.

Tudor style: Style derived from the court architecture of the Tudor period (1485–1603); characterised by the Tudor arch, patterned brickwork, steep roofs and tall, decorated chimneys.

Turret: A very small tower.

Undercroft: A cellar or storage room, often brick-lined and divided by columns that support vaults. Medieval undercrofts were often constructed partly below ground and survive more often than the contemporary houses above them (as at Ladye Place p. 41). Their distribution is irregular, but undercrofts are common in Chester, Southampton, Winchester and London – suggesting, perhaps, that they were a feature of coastal and river towns.[73] Famously, an undercroft beneath the House of Lords in the Old Palace of Westminster was leased to Gunpowder Plot conspirators.

Vault: An architectural term describing an arched ceiling construction, usually of stone. The term is also used to describe an underground room or chamber, especially when vaulted (a burial vault, for example).

Vaulted: See Vault.

Vernacular: A building constructed of locally available materials.

Wainscot: Originally referred to fine-quality quartered oak, with wainscoting being the panels made from it. From the eighteenth century, the term 'wainscot' came to refer to panelling on the lower parts of walls.

Wainscoting: See Panelling and Wainscot.

Wars of the Three Kingdoms: A series of interrelated armed conflicts in England (including Wales), Scotland and Ireland between 1639 and 1651, of which the best known are the English Civil War (1642–51) and the Scottish Civil War (1644–45).

APPENDIX:
A GREAT ESCAPE

The story of Charles II's escape from the Battle of Worcester is a fast-paced thriller. Defeated by Cromwell's New Model Army in 1651, he spent six weeks on the run before fleeing to France until his restoration in 1660. The route is easily traced – there is even a long-distance footpath called 'The Monarch's Way'.

Charles had many adventures and, fortunately for him, Royalist-aligned Roman Catholics had been keeping secrets and hiding people since Elizabethan times.

Diary Notes
3 Sept, 1651, Worcester: Charles flees the Battle of Worcester after his 16,000 mainly Scottish forces are overwhelmed by Cromwell's much larger New Model Army. Charles (accompanied by Lord Derby, Lord Wilmot, Charles Giffard and others) is talked out of going to London and shadows the fleeing Scots Cavalry. It is soon clear that the large body of men will attract unwanted attention:

> ... we had such a number of beaten men with us, of the horse, that I strove, as soon as ever it was dark, to get from them; and though I could not get them to stand by me against the enemy, I could not get rid of them, now I had a mind to it.

Giffard persuades Charles to go to his Boscobel Estate on the Staffordshire–Shropshire border.
4 Sept, White Ladies Priory: Charles arrives at the former priory[74] in the early hours and the party splits up. He is taken in by the tenants, the Pendrells, and quickly 'divested of his apparell, his hayr cut off, and habited like a country fellow'.
4 Sept, Spring Coppice: Accompanied by Richard Pendrell ('Trusty Dick'), the king hides in Spring Coppice wood.[75] They are within sight of the highway, and Charles observes passing militia. He later recalled, 'In this wood I stayed all day without meat or drink and by great fortune it rained all the time which

hindered them, as I believe, from coming into the wood to search for men that might be fled there.'

He resolves to head for largely Royalist Wales, rather than London, and assumes the alias of 'Will Jones', a woodsman.

5 Sept, Madeley: Charles hopes it will be possible to cross into Wales. After a meal at Hubbal Grange,[76] Charles and Pendrell head for Madeley, near the River Severn. The hour is late, and as they walk past Evelith Mill,[77] the miller challenges them. Charles recalled:

> Just as we came to the mill, we could see the miller, as I believe, sitting at the mill door, he being in white clothes, it being a very dark night. He called out, 'Who goes there?' Upon which Richard Pendrell answered, 'neighbours going home,' or some such-like words. Whereupon the miller cried out, 'If you be neighbours, stand, or I will knock you down.' Upon which, we believing there was company in the house, the fellow bade me follow him close, and he run to a gate that went up a dirty lane, up a hill, and opening the gate, the miller cried out, 'Rogues ! rogues!' And thereupon some men came out of the mill after us, which I believe were soldiers: so we fell a-running, both of us up the lane, as long as we could run, it being very deep and very dirty, till at last I bade him leap over a hedge, and lie still to hear if anybody followed us; which we did, and continued lying down upon the ground about half an hour, when, hearing nobody come, we continued our way on to the village upon the Severn.

It later transpired that the miller was a Royalist ... and had been sheltering Royalist troops.

They reach Madeley around midnight and go to Upper House,[78] the home of a Mr. Francis Wolfe, a firm Royalist. Charles learns that the Severn's crossings are heavily guarded and the secret hiding places at Upper House have been discovered. As a consequence, Charles spends the night in Upper House Barn, hidden in hay.

6 Sept, Boscobel Wood: The plan to cross into Wales is abandoned. Charles and Pendrell return to Boscobel House (see p. 88), and Charles spends the day hiding in a nearby oak with a refugee from Worcester, a Colonel Carlos.

6 Sept, Boscobel House: After dark the pair slip back into the house and Charles spends the night in one of Boscobel's priest holes.

7 Sept, Pendeford Mill: Charles leaves for Moseley Old Hall on Humphrey Pendrell's ageing mill horse, accompanied by five Pendrell brothers and Charles Giffard's servant, Francis Yates. They soon realise the horse cannot go on and stop at Pendeford Mill.[79] Humphrey jokes that the horse has 'the weight of three kingdoms' on its back. Charles continues with two of the Pendrell brothers and Francis Yates.

7 Sept, Moseley Old Hall: Arrive at Moseley Old Hall (p. 102), the home of Thomas Whitgreave (a move arranged by Lord Wilmot, who had taken sanctuary there while Charles was travelling to Madeley). A Roman Catholic priest, Father John Huddlestone, bathes Charles' feet and he sleeps in a bed for the first time since 3 September. On Tuesday 9 September, troops arrive and question Whitgreave about whether he fought for the Royalists at Worcester – (he had not; few had rallied to the king). Convinced of his innocence, they leave.

10 Sept, Bentley Hall: Moseley is no longer safe. Charles moves to Bentley Hall,[80] the home of Colonel John Lane, a Royalist officer. Convicted recusants require a pass to travel more than 8km (5 miles) from their home and Lane's sister, Jane, has been given one to travel with a manservant to visit a pregnant friend in Somerset. A plot is hatched to reach the port of Bristol. 'Will Jones' becomes 'Will Jackson', a neighbouring tenant farmer's son. Charles rides out on the same horse as Jane Lane, accompanied by Withy Petre (Jane's sister), her husband, John, and Henry Lascelles, another Royalist officer. As a decoy, an undisguised Lord Wilmot rides ahead of the party. If challenged, he will say he is out hunting.

10 Sept, Bromsgrove: The horse loses a shoe and Charles goes to get another. Charles talks with a blacksmith, a conversation he related to the diarist, Samuel Pepys:

> As I was holding my horse's foot, I asked the smith what news. He told me that there was no news that he knew of, since the good news of the beating the rogues of the Scots. I asked him whether there was none of the English taken that joined with the Scots, He answered he did not hear if that rogue, Charles Stuart, were taken; but some of the others, he said, were taken, but not Charles Stuart. I told him that if that rogue were taken, he deserved to be hanged more than all the rest, for bringing in the Scots. Upon which he said I spoke like an honest man; and so we parted.

Sept 10, Wootton Wawen: They see Parliamentarian troops ahead. Fearful of being accosted, Mr and Mrs Petre take an alternative route to Stratford-upon-Avon. Charles, Jane and Henry ride through the troops, unhindered.

Sept 10, Long Marston: Still disguised as a manservant, Charles stays at the home of one of Jane's kinsmen, a Mr Tomes. The cook puts Charles to work in the kitchen, winding up a meat-roasting jack in the fireplace. He struggles with the task, and the cook asks. 'What countryman are you, that you know not how to wind up a jack?'[81]

Charles explains, 'I am a poor tenant's son of Colonel Lane's in Staffordshire. We seldom have roast meat, but when we have, we don't make use of a jack.' The explanation is accepted.

11 Sept, Cirencester: They stay the night at an inn, thought to have been The Crown on the corner of Black Jack Street.[82]

12 Sept, Abbots Leigh: The group arrive at the house[83] of the Norton family, friends of the Lanes. Charles' identity is kept secret for the three days (to keep a low profile, he pretends to be unwell). Charles asks a servant who claimed to have served with the Royalists at Worcester to describe the king. He replies, 'the king was at least three fingers taller [than you]'. At one point, Mrs Norton passes by and Charles respectfully removes his hat. A servant named Pope looks 'very earnestly' at his face.

Pope, it transpires, had worked in the royal household when Charles was a boy, and had been a trooper in his father's army. On being told that Pope suspected he was the king, and that he could be trusted, Charles reveals his true identity. He tasks Pope with going to Bristol to determine whether there were any ships to Spain or France. That night, Pope reports that there are no ships for at least a month, and recommends that Charles and Lord Wilmot go to Trent, the home of the staunch Royalist, Francis Wyndham.

16 Sept, Castle Carey: Early that morning, Charles and Wilmot move to the manor house at Castle Carey.[84]

17 Sept, Trent: Arrive at Francis Wyndham's home, Trent House.[85] Over the next few days, Wilmot and Wyndham (the latter calling himself Captain Norris) seek a ship sailing from Weymouth or Lyme Regis. Via a sea captain named William Ellesdon they book passage from Lyme Regis with a Captain Limbry. At Trent, Charles hears church bells and sees people gathered in the churchyard making bonfires. A maid tells him they are celebrating because a rogue trooper from Cromwell's army claimed he had killed the king, and was wearing his coat. Mrs Lane and Lassells return home.

22 Sept, Charnmouth: Charles rides with Juliana Coningsby (Lady Wyndham's niece) to Charnmouth, pretending to be a runaway bridal party from Devonshire (Wilmot plays the husband, Charles their manservant). They go to the Queen's Arms Inn[86] and wait for Captain Limbry. He fails to arrive. Later, Limbry claims his wife locked him in a room after learning that he intended to take a group of Royalists to France.

23 Sept, Bridport: The group continues to Bridport to meet Wilmot. They find it swarming with Parliamentarian troops, but Charles proceeds to the George Inn,[87] leading the horses straight through a mass of annoyed troopers and into the inn's stable. The hostler strikes up a conversation with Charles, claiming he had surely seen his face before. Charles remains calm. After drawing out of the hostler that he had lived at an Exeter inn near a Mr Potter, he tells him that he worked under Mr Potter for over a year. They part with a promise to drink a pot of beer together. Charles talks freely to the troopers, pretending to be waiting on them at dinner. As a precaution, the party move on.

23 Sept, Broadwindsor: The night is spent at The Castle Inn.[88] Their host shows the party to their lodgings in the attic, 'where privateness recompensed the meanness of the accommodation, and the pleasantness of the host (a merry fellow) allayed and mitigated the weariness of the guests'. The party's mood brightens – but not for long. The local constable arrives with forty soldiers on their way to Jersey. They are to be billeted there for the night and take up all the lower rooms. The king feels 'besieged'. Fortunately, one of the women travelling with the soldiers goes into labour and an argument breaks out. In the resulting melee, Charles escapes.

24 Sept, Trent: The party returns to the relative safety of Trent House. They spend the next few weeks there while they seek passage to France. Passage is secured aboard a ship from Southampton on 29 September, but it is commandeered by troops bound for Jersey.

5 Oct, Heale House: Charles heads for Heale House,[89] accompanied by Juliana Conningsby and Henry Peters (Colonel Wyndham's servant). The king spends his days at Stonehenge, returning to the house after dark. On 7 October, Wilmot secures passage on a small coal-brig named *Surprise* from Shoreham, near Brighton, for the sum of £60. It is captained by a Nicholas Tattersall.

14 Oct, Brighton: The party spends the night at the George Inn, Brighton,[90] where the drunken proprietor recognises the king:

> ... just as he was looking about, and saw there was nobody in the room, he, upon a sudden, kissed my hand that was upon the back of the chair, and said to me, 'God bless you wheresoever you go! I do not doubt, before I die, but to be a lord, and my wife a lady.' So I laughed, and went away into the next room, not desiring then any further discourse with him.

Later, Captain Tattersall realises who he will be carrying and increases his fee to £200.

15 Oct, Shoreham: Charles sets sail for northern France. Hours after he sails, a group of Parliamentarian cavalry troops arrive in Shoreham to arrest him.

16 Oct, Fécamp: Charles and Lord Wilmot land in Fécamp. The next day they travel to Rouen, and then on to Paris to stay with the king's mother, Henrietta Maria. Charles does not return to England for nine years.

He returns a changed man. Many who helped him are rewarded, and on his deathbed in 1685, the king converts to Catholicism.

Notes for Investigators

1 Scott, 1830, pp. 333–34. Scott describes crossing the crypt and 'had an idea of the vicinity of the Castle Chapel'. Architectural historian Gordon Slade thus suggests Scott stayed in the room beneath the Chapel (the Blue Room). However, the Rev. John Stirton, in his book *Glamis: A Parish History*, published in 1913, contradicts Slade's assertion by stating that:

> From the Billiard-Room [above the great kitchen on the second floor] we retrace our steps, and crossing the banqueting hall and ascending the great staircase in the tower, we come to a passage which leads among others to the room that Sir Walter Scott occupied when he spent the night at Glamis.

2 Wood, 1936, p. 27.
3 Ibid, p. 33. Augusta Maclagan – the 12th Earl's sister-in-law – wrote to Lord Halifax in the 1870s.
4. Ibid, p. 26.
5 Slade, 2000, p. 78. See also Vincent, 1984, pp. 86–87.
6 Vincent, 1984, p. 87.
7 Whitegate, Northwich, Cheshire CW8 2BA. Medieval abbey, and following the Dissolution, a country house built for the Holcrofts. From the seventeenth century, Vale Royal was the seat of the Cholmondeley family. Now a private golf club, wedding and events venue.
8 See Miller, 1890, p. 64 and pp. 67–68. The current Glamis Castle archivist, Ingrid Thompson, communicated to the author that there was a small charter room in the old palace, now part of the private apartments and directly under the Queen Mother's Bedroom (in the south-east wing). The archives were kept in that room until the early 1970s and this was, presumably, the room shown to royal biographer Michael Thornton. The castle manager, Tom Baxter, believes that these were the rooms used by the 3rd Earl's wife, Helen Middleton.
9 Slade, 2000, p. 42 and p. 62. See also Apted, 1986.
10 Wood, 1936, p.27 Neither the current castle manager nor the castle archivist have heard of any stones with iron rings in any of the bedroom cupboards (pers comm., in 2015).
11 Not open to the public.
12 Not open to the public .

13 See Morris, 1872 and 1881, Jardine, 1857 and Caraman, 1952.

14 Quoted in Morris, 1872, p. 188.

15 Quoted in Morris, 1872, pp. 182–84.

16 Reminiscent of Aston Hall, Birmingham (p. 102), this famous priest-harbouring centre was pulled down and rebuilt following a fire in the nineteenth century. In 1606, an eight-day search involving 100 men uncovered eleven of Nicholas Owen's priest holes. Owen himself was taken in the search, along with the Jesuit priests Henry Garnet and Edward Oldcorne.

17 *State Papers Domestic, Elizabeth*, vol. CCXLIII, no. 95.

18 Chenies, Buckinghamshire, WD3 6ER. House and gardens open part year.

19 Not open to the public.

20 Not open to the public.

21 Skirlaugh, East Yorkshire HU11 4LN. Open part year.

22 Welbeck, Worksop, Nottinghamshire S80 3LW. Summer tours of Welbeck Abbey State Rooms.

23 Church Lane, West Wycombe, High Wycombe, Buckinghamshire HP14 3AH. Open all year.

24 See 'Priest's Hiding Places, etc.', *Notes and Queries*, vol. 12 (306), 8 September, 1855, p. 191. Chelvey Court has since been converted into two apartments. A square, ashlar porch bears the arms of John Tynte who, along with his father Edward, built the house between 1618 and 1660 on the site of an earlier property. The house retains fragments of seventeenth-century panelling and doors.

There were said to be two priest holes here, perhaps retained as insurance against the family's Royalist sympathies during the Civil War (John was a Cavalier). One was entered through the panel in the Blue Room on the first floor. The other was under the floor of a cupboard, and was entered via a trapdoor. The latter hide was described as a narrow room with a small window and an iron candle holder projecting from the wall. Fea (1901) wrote:

> Both the panel and the trap-door are now done away with, and the tradition of the existence of secret rooms almost forgotten, though not long since we received a letter from an antiquarian who had seen them thirty years before, and who was actually entertaining the idea of making practical investigations with the aid of a carpenter or mason, to which, as suggested, we were to be party.

The plan was never carried out. It seems likely that the antiquarian was the 'W.A.', who wrote to *Notes and Queries*.

From 1985 and 2000 architect Keith Hallett oversaw a major project that saw the main house converted into two properties. At the request of the author, he kindly provided the following information:

> There was an old cupboard, about 12–13 inches wide, alongside one of the kitchen fireplaces with a cunning drawer in the bottom, below a lockable door. The top of the drawer was rebated as was the bottom of the door above. So the locked door prevented the drawer being opened.
>
> I imagine the drawer may have been for salt … being close to the fireplace. Incidentally it's the meat fireplace, with spit rack above and eye for the crane still evident.
>
> I mention the cupboard because it was built in with timber sides and back. The room was tongue & groove clad up to a shoulder height rail (softwood late Victorian or twentieth century tongue & groove). This was beetle infested and

thoroughly undeserving so it went in our first wave of work. The cupboard was good (although it looked to be an elm door) but it needed to be taken out to eradicate any infestation. We found that the whole cupboard slid out, revealing a small space behind, lime plastered and with a stone floor. An amount of cellulose – no doubt old straw – was on the floor.

This was a very small space but enough to for a person to sit in. Warm, by the fire, easy to get into (although the cupboard was 3ft off the kitchen floor), cunningly concealed – and locked.

I have always thought that this might have been a hiding place for someone loyal to the king during the Civil War before the Commonwealth. There's no doubt that this part of the kitchen range is around 1630–40 so this speculation of mine would make sense.

As to the priest hole, in the older part of the house at first floor (living areas next to the 'Blue Room' there is a cupboard with old floorboards. The boards are loose and there is a space below. This is on what would have been an external wall before the kitchen range was added, when the house was a single room in depth.

I prefer to think that this cupboard was a garderobe. There is a formed slot in what would have been the outside wall which relates to the cupboard. The slot appears to offer a place for defecating on to the ground below. There's no evidence of any windows nearby on this west facing wall.

The panelling in the Blue Room is intact. Careful inspection by HBMC people in 1985 suggests that this panelling and highly decorative stone fire surround (combining strap work with early Renaissance detailing) is likely to have been moved from elsewhere in the house.

25 Not open to the public.
26 See 'Priest's Hiding Places, etc.', *Notes and Queries*, vol. 12 (296), 21 July 1855, p. 48
27 Not open to the public.
28 Not open to the public.
29 Not open to the public.
30 Not open to the public.
31 Not open to the public.
32 Broadclyst, Exeter, Devon EX5 3LE. National Trust. Open part year.
33 Norwich, Norfolk NR11 8PR. National Trust. Open part year.
34 Grantham, Leicestershire, NG32 1PE. Open part year.
35 Not open to the public. The statue that operated the mechanism has been removed and the door is no longer concealed.
36 Not open to the public. Occasionally, the owners host events within the grounds.
37 A Dorset antiquarian alerted historian Granville Squires to the discovery, the story of which appeared in his 1934 book, *Secret Hiding Places*.
38 Clarendon, 1888, pp. 189–90.
39 Maxwell Lyte, 1909, p. 177.
40 For further information, see Rivers-Moore's reports of 1934 and 1938.
41 *State Papers Domestic, Elizabeth*, vol. CXCIII, no. 17.
42 Bulwer-Lytton, 1883, p. 29.
43 Ibid, p. 26.
44 See Morris, 1872, pp. 187–215.
45 The manor house was located near Preston Road Tube Station, Brent, London.
46 See 'The Manor House, Byfleet' *Surrey Archaeological Collections* 20 (1907), pp. 153–63.
47 In his *Autobiography*. See Morris, 1881 and 1872; and Caraman, 1952.

48 Dry Drayton, Cambridgeshire CB23 8BA. Hosts events and garden open days

49 See Jessop, 1913, p. 180.

50 For further information see Menuge, 2006, p. 55.

51 Not open to the public. The famous 'Plot Room' above the Gatehouse is where the conspirators, led by religious zealot, Robert Catesby, hatched their plan to blow up Parliament with the help of York-born mercenary, Guy Fawkes. At the time, the room had a secret exit.

52 See Hughes, 1857, for the various accounts.

53 True or not, a royal pardon was granted to Nicholas Brome by Henry VII for all crimes, misdemeanours, etc. committed before 7 May 1496 (now kept at Shakespeare's Birthplace Trust, Stratford-upon Avon).

54 Jardine, 1857, pp. 183–84.

55 Gerrard, in Morris, 1872, p. 38.

56 *State Papers Domestic, James I*, vol. XIX, no. 11. Letter from Henry Garnet to Anne Vaux. The full letter, which describes in detail the conditions in his hiding place at Hindlip Hall, can be found in Jardine, 1857, pp. 323–30.

57 Letter from John Bird to Sir Robert Cecil. From Cecil Papers, Calendar of the Cecil Papers in Hatfield House, vol. 9 (1599) 11 January.

58 Wrote Bristol-born Jesuit Father William Warfard in a manuscript entitled *An Account of Several English Martyrs*. Written around 1597, the manuscript is in Father Christopher Greene's collection at Stonyhurst College. Quoted in Camm, 1914, p. 213.

59 Callum, T.G. 'A synopsis of two tours made in Wales in 1775 and in 1811', *Y Cymroder. The Magazine of the Honourable Society for Cymmrodorion*, vol. 38. (London: Issued by the Society, 1927) p. 72.

60 Usk, Monmouthshire NP15 2BT. Open all year.

61 Not open to the public.

62 Great Cillwch, Pitt House and Ty Mawr are not open to the public. For Treowen, see p. 141.

63 Not open to the public.

64 Cwmbran, Torfaen NP44 3YJ. Visits by arrangement.

65 Converted to flats following a fire.

66 Now a restaurant.

67 Neither property is open to the public.

68 Lockhart, 1837, p. 116.

69 Not open to the public.

70 Ellon, Aberdeenshire AB41 7LP. Open part year.

71 Aberfeldy, Perthshire PH15 2JD. Open part year.

72 Not open to the public.

73 Emery, 2012, pp. 156–57.

74 Albrighton, Wolverhampton WV8 1QZ (ruin). English Heritage. Open all year.

75 Monarch's Way passes Spring Coppice (Ordnance Survey grid reference SJ 837 072) south of Boscobel House.

76 Monarch's Way passes the remains of Hubbal Grange or 'Pendrell's Cot', Tong (Ordnance Survey grid reference SJ 814 079). The picturesque, timber-framed cottage was demolished in the 1960s.

77 Monarch's Way passes the site of Evelith Mill at Ordnance Survey grid reference SJ 743 050.

78 Upper House was built for Francis Woolfe around 1621 and must have had a number of secret hiding places. It has three storeys and today contains what could be the remains of a priest hole with a bench in a corner of the attic. Upper House Barn can be found to the north-west of the house. At present, neither building is open to the public.

79 Pendeford Mill Local Nature Reserve, Wolverhampton, Staffordshire WV9 5ET. Open all year.
80 Demolished.
81 King's Lodge, Long Marston (private house). The original roasting jack has been removed.
82 Still a pub.
83 Demolished.
84 Demolished.
85 Not open to the public. The king's hiding place and the rooms in which he is alleged to have stayed have been preserved through the centuries, despite many alterations. The hide is located in the projecting wing over the old brew house, in Lady Anne Wyndam's old room (which writer Sir Frederick Treves described as 'beautifully panelled with black oak' and with 'massive ceiling beams, quaint recesses and secret cupboards for hiding valuables'). He was referring to a shallow space behind the panelling to the right of the fireplace, perhaps used for Mass equipment or prohibited books. Adjoining this room is a small closet entered via an original oak-framed doorway. Part of the floor has a hinged (modern) trapdoor, providing access to a 1.5m square, 70cm deep space that Father Blount said had been 'long before made by some of the ancient family of the Gerards ... who were recusants'. It seems the double floor here is a consequence of the projecting wing being constructed at a different level to the main house. It is recorded that the king resorted to the hiding place at least once when a troop of horses passed nearby. Memorials to Sir Francis and Lady Wyndham can be found in the thirteenth-century church.
86 Still a pub.
87 Probably 9 East Street, Bridport. In 2015 it was a shop.
88 Rebuilt following a fire in the nineteenth century and renamed The George Inn.
89 Middle Woodford, Salisbury, Wiltshire SP4 6NT. Gardens open to the public.
90 Believed to have stood on the site of the King's Head, West Street.

Sources and
Further Reading

In addition to the sources below, much use was made of Pevsner Architectural Guides, Victoria County History guides, *Country Life* magazine, archaeological and listed building reports and numerous visitor guides produced by the National Trust, English Heritage etc., as well as those produced by charitable trusts and private owners.

For in-depth information on priest holes and post-Reformation Roman Catholic families, see Hodgett's *Secret Hiding Places* and the journal *Recusant History*.

Among free to use online resources, the Gunpowder Plot Society's website (www.gunpowder-plot.org) has much to recommend it.

Ainsworth, W.H., *Boscobel; or, The Royal Oak, a Tale of the Year 1651* (London: G. Routledge, 1878)

Apted, M.R., 'The building and other works of Patrick, 1st Earl of Strathmore at Glamis, 1651–1695', *Antiquaries Journal*, 66 (1984) pp. 91–115

Aveling, J.C.H., *The Handle and the Axe: The Catholic Recusants in England from Reformation to Emancipation* (London: Blond and Briggs, 1976)

Barber, C. (ed.), *Hando's Gwent*, vol. 2 (Llanfoist: Blorenge Books, 1989)

Bereton, H.L., *Gordonstoun. Ancient Estate and Modern School* (Edinburgh: R. and R. Clark Ltd, 1968)

Blundell, O., *Ancient Catholic Homes of Scotland* (London: Burns & Oates Ltd, 1907)

Blundell, O., *Old Catholic Lancashire*, vol. 1 (London: Burns & Oates Ltd, 1925)

Brown, R.A., *Allen Brown's English Castles* (Woodbridge: Boydell Press, 2004)

Brown, S., *Boscobel and its Visitors: Recollections by the Custodian* (London: Whitehead Brothers, 1910)

Bulwer-Lytton, Edward Robert (ed.), *The Life, Letters and Literary Remains of Edward Bulwer, Lord Lytton, by his Son*, vol. 1 (London: Keegan Paul, 1883)

Camm, B., *Lives of the English Martyrs*, vol. 1 (London: Longmans, Green & Co., 1914)

Caraman, P., *Henry Garnet, 1555–1606, and the Gunpowder Plot* (New York: Farrar, Straus & Company, 1964)

Caraman, P. (ed.), *The Autobiography of a Hunted Priest* (New York: Pellegrini & Cudahy, 1952)

Carew, R., (1602) *The Survey of Cornwall* (Penryn: Tor Mark Press, Reprinted 2000)

Clarendon, E.H., *History of the Rebellion and Civil Wars in England*, vol. 5, ed. Macray, W.D. (Oxford: Clarendon Press, 1888)

Clark. J. and Jack, S., *Castle Sinclair Girnigoe Conservation Plan*, 2 vols (Field Archaeological Services, 2003)

Emery, A., *Discovering Medieval Houses* (Oxford: Shire Publications Ltd, 2012)

Emery, A., *Greater Medieval Houses of England and Wales 1300–1500*, 3 vols (Cambridge: Cambridge University Press, 2000)

Fea, A., *Secret Chambers and Hiding Places* (London: S.H. Bousfield & Co., 1901)

Fraser, A., *The Gunpowder Plot: Terror And Faith in 1605* (London: Phoenix, 2002)

Gerard, J., 'A Narrative of the Gunpowder Plot', in Morris. J. (ed.), *The Condition of Catholics under James I* (London: Longmans, Green & Co., 1872)

Hodgetts, M., *Secret Hiding Places* (Dublin: Veritas, 1989)

Hughes, J., *The Boscobel Tracts: Relating to the Escape of Charles the Second after the Battle of Worcester and his Subsequent Adventures* (Edinburgh and London: William Blackwood and Sons, 1857)

Hussey, E., 'Scotney Castle', *Archaeologia Cantiana*, vol. 17 (1887) pp. 38–45

Hutchinson, P.O., *A New Guide to Sidmouth and the Neighbourhood* (Sidmouth: Thomas Perry, 1857)

Jardine, D., *A Narrative of the Gunpowder Plot* (London: John Murray, 1857)

Jessop, A., *One Generation of a Norfolk House: A Contribution to Elizabethan History* (London: T. Fisher Unwin, 1913)

Ladlam, H., *The Restless Ghosts of Ladye Place and Other True Hauntings* (London: W. Foulsham & Co. Ltd, 1967)

Lockhart, J.G., *Memoirs of the Life of Sir Walter Scott, Bart*, vol. 4 (Edinburgh: Robert Cadell, 1837)

Macaulay, T.B., (1848) *Macaulay's History of England from the Accession of James II*, vol. 2 (London: J.M. Dent & Sons Ltd, Reprinted 1956)

MacCulloch, D., *Reformation: Europe's House Divided 1490–1700* (London: Penguin, 2004)

MacGibbon, D. and Ross, T., *The Castellated and Domestic Architecture of Scotland from the Twelfth to the Eighteenth Century*, vol. 2 (Edinburgh: David Douglas, 1887)

Malan, A.H., *More Famous Homes of Great Britain and their Stories* (New York: G.P. Putnam's Sons, 1900).

Maxwell Lyte, H.C., *A History of Dunster and the Families of Mohun & Luttrell* (London: The St Catherine Press Ltd, 1909)

Menuge, A., *A Survey and Investigation of the Moated House. Oxburgh Hall, Oxborough, Norfolk*, English Heritage Research Department Report Series, 22, 2006

Miller, A.H. (ed.) The book of record, a diary written by Patrick, First Earl of Strathmore and other documents relating to Glamis Castle, 1684–1689 (Edinburgh: T. and A. Constable, 1890)

Morgan, O. and Wakeman, M., *Notes on the Ancient Domestic Residences of Pentre-Bach, Crick, Ty-Mawr, The Garn, Crindau, and St. Julians* (Newport: Henry Mulloch, 1860)

Morris, J., *The Troubles of our Catholic Forefathers as Related by themselves*, vol. 1 (London: Burns and Oates, 1872)

Morris, J. (ed.)., *The Life of Father John Gerard, of the Society of Jesus* (London: Burns and Oates, 1881)

Moss, F., *Pilgrimages to Old Homes* (Didsbury: The Old Parsonage, 1908)

Peck, F., *Memoirs of the Life and Actions of Oliver Cromwell* (London: [s.n.], 1740)

Priestly, J., *Eltham Palace* (Chichester: Phillmore & Co. Ltd, 2008)

Prince, J., *Danmonii Orientales Illustres: Or, the Worthies of Devon* (Exeter: C. Yeo and P. Bishop, 1701)

Rivers-Moore, C.N., 'Excavations at St. Mary's Priory, Hurley: Second Report', *Berkshire Archaeological Journal*, 42, (1938) pp.23–30

Rivers-Moore, C.N., 'Recent discoveries at St. Mary's Priory, Hurley', *Berkshire Archaeological Journal*, 38 (1934) pp.7–17

Robinson, J.M., *Arundel Castle* (Chichester: Phillimore & Co. Ltd, 1994)

Ross, S., *History in Hiding* (London: Robert Hale Ltd, 1991)

Scott, W., *Letters on Witchcraft and Demonology* (London: John Murray, 1830)

Sharp, M.A., *The History of Ufton Court and the Parish of Ufton, in the County of Berks and of the Perkins Family* (London: Elliott Stock, 1892)

Slade, H.G., 'Castle Fraser, a seat of the ancient family of Fraser', *Proceedings of the Society of Antiquaries of Scotland*, 109 (1989) pp.233–98

Slade, H.G., *Glamis Castle* (London: Society of Antiquaries, London, 2000)

Somerset Fry, P., *The David & Charles Book of Castles* (Newton Abbot: David & Charles, 1980)

Squires, G., *Secret Hiding Places* (London: S. Paul & Co., 1934)

Stirton, J., *Glamis: a Parish History* (Forfar: W. Shepherd, 1913)

Taylor, H., *Old Halls in Lancashire and Cheshire. Including Notes on the Ancient Domestic Architecture of the Counties Palatine* (Manchester: J.E. Cornish, 1884)

The Tragic Legend of Salford Hall in the County of Warwickshire (Redditch: Frank Donald Ltd, 1968)

Thornton, M., *Royal Feud: The Queen Mother and the Duchess of Windsor* (London: Michael Joseph, 1985)

Treves, F., *Highways and Byways in Dorset* (London: Macmillan and Co., 1914)

Vincent, J. (ed.), *The Crawford Papers: The Journals of David Lindsay, Twenty-Seventh Earl of Crawford and Tenth Earl of Balcarres during the Years 1892 to 1940* (Manchester: Manchester University Press, 1984)

Wentworth-Day, J., *The Queen Mother's Family Story* (London: Robert Hale, 1967)

Wood, C.L., 2nd Viscount Halifax, *Lord Halifax's Ghost Book* (London: Geoffrey Bless, 1936)

Wood, G.B., *Secret Britain: A Tourist's Collection of Hides, Ghosts and Stratagems* (London: Cassell, 1968)

SOURCES AND FURTHER READING

Author's Acknowledgements

In particular I wish to acknowledge the information and assistance I have received in researching this book from the following individuals: John Wheelock, Ingrid Thompson, Rachel Hunt, Jeff Griffiths, Julie Hutton, Briony Carter and the staff at the Salford Hall Hotel, the staff at Billesley Manor, Ruth Poyner, Sherida Breedon, Mimi Mzari, Robert Tucker, Tom Baxter, Ingrid Nicholas, Mike Durnan, Keith Hallett, Dr John Martin Robinson, Dr Neil Rushton, Bob Hayword and Mme Elodie Bady.

I would also like to thank Nicola Guy, Declan Flynn, Sophie Bradshaw and Juanita Hall at The History Press for their patience and support and likewise, my family.

The following illustrations are reproduced by kind permission of the individuals and institutions below:

P. 2 Courtesy of the Earl of Strathmore and Kinghorne, p. 30 Courtesy of the National Trust, Cotehele, p. 33 Carol Allerton, p. 35 and p. 36 Columbia Photography / John Haworth, p. 45, p. 46 and p. 47 Courtesy of Ufton Court Educational Trust, p. 57, Marion Smith (www.marionsmithdrawings.com), p. 58 Robert Tucker, p. 63 and p. 64 Julie Hutton, p. 66 Michelham Priory, p. 67 Michelham Priory / Karl Herdman, p. 68 Arundel Castle Trustees Ltd, p. 69 Arundel Castle Trustees Ltd / Paul Barker, p. 71 Courtesy of Chichester Cathedral, p. 88 English Heritage, p. 92 and p. 95 The National Trust, p. 101 Courtesy of Billesley Manor, p. 108 (bottom), p. 113, p. 115 (top), p. 116 (bottom right) Courtesy of Harvington Hall (www.harvingtonhall.com), p. 124 Courtesy of Sam Litten and Borwick Hall Education Centre, p. 135 Chris Chambers, p. 136 Courtesy of Hazelwood Castle, p. 149 Scottish Viewpoint / Craig Brown, p. 165 and 166 (top) Jean-Baptiste Bady, p. 166 (bottom) Mme Elodie Bady.

Index of Properties and Places

Those entries listed in capital letters correspond to entries found in Amazing Places to Visit and Stay.